WINNING WORDS

THE CREATIVE POWER OF WHAT YOU SAY

MARGARET COURT

Strand Publishing
Sydney

Winning Words: The Creative Power of What You Say

First published 1999 by Strand Publishing

ISBN 187 682 5243

Distributed in Australia by:
Family Reading Publications
B100 Ring Road
Ballarat, Victoria, 3352
Phone: (03) 5334 3244
Fax: (03) 5334 3299
Email: orders@frp.com.au

Edited by Owen Salter
Cover design by Andrew Cunningham
Cover photos used by permission of the Photo Library
Typesetting by Midland Typesetters, Maryborough, Victoria
Printed by Australian Print Group, Maryborough, Victoria

Contents

Acknowledgments iv

The Margaret Court Story 1
Introduction 5

1 The Power of Words 8
2 How Words Affect You 21
3 God's Words 36
4 Words of Faith 49
5 Words for the Heart 62
6 How Words Affect Your Destiny 72
7 Winning Words to Health 85
8 Winning Words to Righteousness 99
9 Winning Words to Peace and Security 116
10 Winning Words for the Battle 129

Some of the Scriptures That Changed My Life 141
The Prayer of Salvation 154

ACKNOWLEDGMENTS

I would like to dedicate this book to the glory of God and thank Him for His constant motivation, direction and inspiration, without Whose help this book would not have been written and I would not be here today.

Additionally I would like to express my thanks to the following people, who with their support, encouragement and unwavering faith in me also brought this book into being:

My husband, Barry, who has supported me and been a constant tower of strength to me.

My children, Daniel, Marika, Teresa and Lisa, who have been a constant encouragement to me.

To all of the people who appear in the pages of this book, who helped to shape my life and destiny in God.

Colin Handreck of Family Reading Publications who continually encouraged me to write yet another book.

David Dixon, Publisher, who has brought everything together so wonderfully.

Owen Salter, editor, whose tireless editing and proofreading has produced such wonderful results.

Barbara Oldfield, one of my dear friends, who tirelessly researched the material for the manuscript.

Jackie Battley, my secretary, for proofreading and post-script corrections.

I pray that as you have a glimpse of what God has done in my life, He can and will do the same in your life. He is no respecter of persons. I also pray that as each person takes hold of God's Word and applies it to every situation, lives will be changed, families will be brought back together, restoration will come, spirit, soul, body, financially and socially, and that people are set free to become all that God wants them to be.

The Margaret Court Story

Margaret Smith Court is one of the greatest tennis players of all time. From hitting a hairless ball with a plank of wood against a garage wall as a child of eight, she progressed to win a total of sixty-two Grand Slam titles in singles, doubles and mixed doubles in a career spanning seventeen years. The Grand Slam itself—the Australian, French, US and Wimbledon titles all in the same year—became hers in 1970, only the second Grand Slam in women's tennis history.

Born in 1942 into a working class family, Margaret began her career sneaking through a hole in the hedge of the Albury tennis club in New South Wales, Australia. Such was her talent, however, that the club professional, Wally Rutter, eventually took her under his arm and provided free coaching. At about thirteen years of age she came to the attention of legendary Australian player and coach Frank Sedgeman, who sowed the seed in her mind that she could be the first Australian woman to win Wimbledon.

The Australian Open was her first major title, won at age seventeen in 1960. Joining the international circuit in 1961, she became one of the top four players on her first tour. Despite susceptibility to nerves and an acrimonious split with tennis officials in Australia, she won the Australian, French and American championships in her second year, but lost Wimbledon to a young American player, Billie Jean King. The following year she defeated King and took the title, the first of three Wimbledon singles crowns. Her 1970 final against King, which Margaret won 14–12, 11–9, is legendary.

In 1965 Margaret won her seventh successive Australian Open and again came close to her first Grand Slam, losing only the French Open. But by 1966, 'The Arm' (as Billie Jean called her in deference to her hitting power) had had enough. She retired at just twenty-four years of age. Two years later, however, with the encouragement of her new husband, Barry Court, she made a comeback. In 1969 she took three-quarters of the Grand Slam for the third time (Wimbledon continuing to be her 'jinxed' tournament) and then finally reached tennis's ultimate achievement in 1970.

When Margaret fell unexpectedly pregnant in 1971, she adopted a new dream: to be the first mother to rank number one in the world. This she achieved after less than a year back on the circuit. She went through 1973 in dominating form, taking three major titles for the fourth time in her career. After having her second child in 1974 she made a second comeback at the age of thirty-three. She won her last major championship, the US Open doubles, in 1975 and retired shortly afterwards.

But towering as her tennis record is, Margaret found that sporting success did not fill the inner hunger that kept her striving for one goal after another. A life-long church attender (she was raised a Catholic), she sat in a church service in Paris during the French Open in 1973, wondering if there was more to knowing God than simply being in church. God was not real or personal to her. That day she prayed that God would reveal Himself to her in a tangible way.

The answer to that prayer came later that year in the US when someone gave her a book, *How to Be Born Again*. Usually religious books ended in the trash can, but Margaret read this one again and again. On returning to Perth she learned that a close friend had become a 'born again' Christian, and shortly afterwards Margaret too gave her life to Christ. She felt as though someone had switched a light on inside. Today she counts this as the most significant day of her life.

Despite her new-found faith, a great sense of inferiority and worthlessness dogged her, along with fear and insecurity. Teaching she received from some Christians stressed the need to be 'healed' from past life hurts, an emphasis, she says, that made her 'totally self-centred' as she constantly analysed her life. 'My self-esteem crumbled. I did not even feel human any more as I cried all the time in a state of emotional distress.' Insomnia and depression grew, and she was diagnosed with a torn heart valve. In 1979 she was hospitalised.

Shortly after, Margaret was given a video tape by a pastor from America, Dr Frederick K. Price. Here, for the first time, she heard that 'confessing' the Word of God was the only way to grow in faith and overcome the defeat in her life. She began to attend a church that taught along similar lines. As she applied what she was learning, she experienced first the complete healing of her heart problem, then the radical transformation of her mental and emotional life.

In 1991 Margaret established Margaret Court Ministries with a vision to bring people to faith in Jesus. As a result of her growing ministry, 1995 saw Victory Life Centre established in Perth. Today it has a congregation of about 700 people and Margaret is the Senior Pastor. The church runs a Bible Training Centre, an Outreach Ministry and a Community Services Program. Sixteen nondenominational churches are affiliated with Victory Life Centre.

Margaret says, 'I have achieved many, many goals, but the greatest thing that has ever happened to me is accepting Jesus Christ'. Today she dedicates her energies to helping others discover God's principles for an abundant and successful life.

Introduction

Words are powerful. They can create or destroy, encourage or discourage, build up or tear down. The power of words is not measured by their volume or the intensity of their delivery, but by their effectiveness in fulfilling their purpose.

Powerful speech flows from an inspired heart, either for good or evil.

An example from history illustrates the point. Sir Winston Churchill, the English war-time Prime Minister, inspired a nation to greatness by using his words to construct a picture of victory in the face of certain defeat. His famous address calling the nation never to surrender turned Britain's darkest hour into arguably its finest. His words created faith in a nation and inspired the whole world to believe that good could triumph over evil.

Alternatively, the dictator Adolph Hitler used his skilful, manipulative way with words to inspire a nation to evil. His words were so powerfully motivated by the appalling intent in his heart that he nearly succeeded in his grandiose scheme of world domination. His words created fear and inspired men to do inconceivable evil on a colossal scale.

The Bible perfectly describes the subtle, devious power of words: *'The words of his mouth were smoother than butter, but war was in his heart; his words were softer than oil, yet they were drawn swords'* (Psalm 55:21).

Endless tapestries of both good and evil can be woven by our words. What we say reveals what is in our hearts. God had the image of the whole creation in His heart before the world ever was, and when He spoke this image into being, His words created exactly what He had within Him, through the awesome power of the Holy Spirit. In Genesis we see time and time again how God spoke the creation into existence: *'Then God said, "Let there be light"; and there was light'* (Genesis 1:3).

Endless tapestries of both good and evil can be woven by our words.

We too create with our words. We bring the things we see in our hearts into being through our mouths, just as God did.

If our words are godly words we will create the lifestyle God wants us to have: heaven here on earth. If our words are not godly they will create the lifestyle the devil wants us to have: hell here on earth. The choice is ours.

Winners don't entertain thoughts or words of defeat. If we want to be winners in life we need to start speaking the way winners speak. The only way we can do that is to find out what God wants us to speak and to concentrate on doing everything He wants us to do.

If we want to be winners in life we need to start speaking the way winners speak.

This book has been written to show why the things we say are so powerful and why we need to change the way we speak. We all need to grow, but if we want change, it will only come as we resolve to change our words.

Chapter 1

The Power of Words

He who guards his mouth preserves his life.
(Proverbs 13:3)

Words determine the shape of our lives. We live today in what we said about ourselves yesterday. Tomorrow we will live in what we say about ourselves today. If we don't like what we are today, we need to change our words.

If we can control our words we can control our whole life.

The Bible shows us that, just as ships can be controlled by small rudders and horses by tiny bridles, we can be controlled by our seemingly small and insignificant tongues.

> *For we all stumble in many things. If anyone does not stumble in word, he is a perfect man, able also to bridle the whole body. Indeed, we put bits in horses' mouths that they may obey us, and we turn their whole body. Look also at ships: although they are so large and are driven by fierce winds, they are turned by a very small rudder wherever the pilot desires. (James 3:2–4)*

As the pilots of our lives, we need to set our mouths

in the right direction. We can't simply turn them loose to say whatever we feel like. Our tongues can set our whole lives on fire. They can corrupt our whole person.

How often have you, like me, wished you had held your tongue? Some reasonably innocent situation flared up into a major disaster, all because of your foolish words. As the Bible says, '*A fool's lips enter into contention, and his mouth calls for blows. A fool's mouth is his destruction, and his lips are the snare of his soul*' (Proverbs 18:6–7).

But words can also do untold good. If the careless use of a rudder sends a ship onto the rocks, wise use steers it through a narrow channel into a safe and peaceful harbour. Just like a yachtsman setting his course with a rudder, we set our course with our mouths. What we say determines both our nature and our life.

THE CREATIVE POWER OF WORDS

There is one simple reason why words have such a powerful effect. Words have enormous creative power.

God created the world with words. When He said, '*Let there be light!*', the Bible tells us light was! And God, who created us in His own image and likeness, put into us the same power to create with the words of our mouths. God framed the world with His words, and we frame our world with our words.

God framed the world with His words, and we frame our world with our words.

By faith we understand that the worlds were framed by the word of God, so that the things which are seen were not made of things which are visible. (Hebrews 11:3)

I have experienced this often in my own life. When I was young, people often asked me what I wanted to do with my tennis. I answered without hesitation, 'I want to be the first Australian woman to win Wimbledon'. This goal was put into my mind by the great tennis coach Frank Sedgeman. Although I was not naturally a confident person, those words drove me towards a goal which eventually became reality.

We have been given a unique ability to create a vision on the inside of us. Champions picture success long before they taste it. Losers picture defeat long before it happens. Success or defeat are birthed in the mind. Our mind needs to be trained to think positive godly thoughts and our mouth needs to release these same thoughts in words so that the vision inside us can become a reality.

When the Bible says that God made us in His image, it means that we are spirit, just as God is. Each of us is a spirit who lives in a body and has a soul (the area of the mind, will and intellect). Since we are really spirit beings, we have been given the same power as God to create any vision we can see in our spirit—through our mouths.

SPEAKING FROM THE HEART

The Bible often refers to our spirit as our 'heart'. If we are not familiar with God and His ways we will have an 'evil heart'. Our spirit will be dead to the things of God, our mind will be negatively programmed by the world and our body will be involved in some form of carnality. If we are familiar with God and His ways we will have a 'good heart'. Our spirit will have come alive to the things of God, our mind will be in the process of being renewed through His Word, and we will be presenting our body daily to the Lord.

Every person speaks from one of these two hearts, either good or evil. Even as Christians we can speak from an evil heart at times. For while our spirit is alive to God, we can still be held captive by our old ways of thinking and acting.

Our words reveal what we are really like in our hearts. A good man will bring out good things from his heart while an evil man will bring out evil. Jesus made this very clear when He said it was not what went into a man that defiled him but what came out of him:

> *Brood of vipers! How can you, being evil, speak good things? For out of the abundance of the heart the mouth speaks. A good man out of the good treasure of his heart brings forth good things, and an evil man out of the evil treasure brings forth evil things. (Matthew 12:34–35)*

As We Think, So We Speak

Our words will always indicate what we are consistently seeing, hearing, thinking and doing. It's impossible to imagine a sports buff who will not find a way to talk about sport. The thing that consumes his thoughts will always find its way out through his mouth.

In fact, every word we speak has its origin in our thoughts. Some thoughts remain no longer than the time it takes to think them, and our ensuing words have little impact. Thoughts like this don't influence us to any great degree. Students everywhere are living examples of this. They cram dozens of ideas into their minds for an examination which are not there a day or two later!

Thoughts that find their way down into our spirit impact us enormously.

On the other hand, thoughts that find their way down into our spirit impact us enormously. Thousands of thoughts invade our space every day. Our minds reject many of these. Not every thought we have is 'conceived' in our imaginations and 'birthed' back through our mouths. But some get down into our hearts, and it's these that have creative power for good or evil when they leave our lips.

We all know by experience how thoughts filter down into our spirit and remain there until the opportunity comes to express them. Generally they come out in fits of emotion—often rage, abuse and anger—when our fuse is lit by some situation we are struggling to handle. We give everyone a piece of our mind, then stand back and say we're sorry because we don't know where it all came from!

The truth is, we do know where it came from. Our mind and emotions have been rehearsing exactly what we would say if given the chance.

PROGRAMMED FOR THE NEGATIVE

When deeply meditated thoughts flow out in words we see the incredible creative power of words at work. What we say both creates and reveals the basic orientation of our lives.

What we say both creates and reveals the basic orientation of our lives.

If we are programmed to the ways of the world we will constantly speak words of negativity and defeat. 'The kids get sick every time we go on holidays.' 'John will probably die like his father at forty with a heart condition.' 'I just know I'll have an accident at that intersection one day.' 'The bank is putting up the fees.' 'I'm sure I'll be the first one laid off the job.' 'No one likes me.' 'I'm ugly.' 'I'm lonely and depressed.'

The amazing thing is that the kids do get sick every holidays, John does suffer a heart attack and the car accident happens, just as we predicted.

We may think being negative is just being realistic, but we are actually creating the very situation we fear. Even before it happens we picture it happening. That picture is so compelling that we really do start to believe it will occur. We are quick to tell everyone who will listen about our fears. We become our own worst enemy, for the things we say will come to pass. We don't want them to come to pass, and we live in hope and pray that they won't. But they do. And they always will, until we change the image of fear in our heart to one of faith and bring our words in line.

Another place we see the power of words is with anxiety. So many people feel, as I once did, that if they could just stop their minds going around and around all the time, thinking on all their worries and anxieties, they would be able to cope. And they are right. *'Anxiety in the heart of man causes depression, but a good word makes it glad'* (Proverbs 12:25).

If our minds are always centred around our worries and fears, those images will be like a stronghold in our hearts. We will find ourselves speaking about our problems all the time to anyone who comes near us. By our words we can make our anxieties so big they are impossible to overcome. *'For a dream comes through much activity, and a fool's voice is known by his many words'* (Ecclesiastes 5:3).

If our minds are always centred around our worries and fears, those images will be like a stronghold in our hearts.

The solution is to change our focus from the problems we face to the answers we truly desire. It takes the same time to speak the positive as it does to speak the negative. It is much better to say, 'The children are always healthy on their holidays', 'My husband is respected and will be promoted at work', 'John will have a long and healthy life', 'I am prosperous'.

But making this change is not easy. Usually we can't speak this way because we don't have the picture of those positive things in our hearts. The only picture we have is the well-developed negative. We are like cameras that can't reproduce a positive picture because our focus is always on the negative.

We may try to suppress our words, somehow knowing we should not be so negative, deceitful, depressed or whatever. But if they come from established attitudes in our hearts we are fighting a losing battle. We have to change our hearts before we can change our words.

CHANGING YOUR HEART

How we can change our hearts and move from negative living to positive living is what this book is about. The most effective way to change your heart is to change your mind to think a different way. The mind is the gateway to the spirit, and whatever gets down into your spirit through your mind will affect every single part of your being.

God tells us in His Word that the way to change our minds is to renew them by the Word of God. Since God's Word is spirit and is totally positive, alive, creative and energising, it's only natural that a consistent diet of such food will produce that image in our hearts. Alternatively, a steady diet of negatives, death, destruction, horror, doom and gloom will produce negative, fear-filled images in our hearts.

It is not enough to determine by an act of our will

that we are going to stop speaking negatively. As every athlete knows, the only way we can stop speaking defeat is to start speaking victory! And the only way to speak victory is to find out what God says and to start saying that. God's Word is absolute truth, so when we speak it we are always speaking what is true.

The only way to speak victory is to find out what God says and to say that.

How do we get the Word of God into our hearts? By confessing it—that is, by saying it aloud—to God, to others and to yourself, until the Holy Spirit establishes it in your heart and your faith rises to embrace it. Speak it out again and again! This is not a gimmick but a principle of faith, because faith, we are told, *'comes by* hearing, *and hearing by the word of God'* (Romans 10:17). When we hear the words of life coming from our mouths, they flow from the Spirit of God into our spirit.

> *It is the Spirit who gives life; the flesh profits nothing. The words that I speak to you are spirit, and they are life. (John 6:63)*

WORDS OF TWO KINGDOMS

Words don't have the luxury of being neutral. They come from one of two realms: the kingdom of light, which is God's kingdom, or the kingdom of darkness, which is Satan's. One is good, the other evil. There is no middle ground.

Words will create either life or death, encouragement or discouragement, peace or strife, health or sickness, blessing or cursing, wealth or poverty, love or hatred.

Every single day we have a choice to make between these two. We can either speak words that produce life and health or words that produce fear and death. We need to deliberately set our mouths in the direction of our desires. If we want healing we can't afford to talk sickness. If we want peace we can't afford to talk about anxieties, cares and worries. If we want success we can't afford to talk defeat.

Every day we have a choice: to speak words that produce life and health, or words that produce fear and death.

God instructs us to choose Him above all else. If we make our choices according to the world's standards, we will be choosing the way of death, because many things which seem right to the world, measured by the yardstick of secular humanism, are very wrong to God. But if we make our choices according to God and His ways, we will be choosing life.

God tells us to obey His Word; the world tells us to rebel against all types of authority and do whatever we want to. God tells us to avoid sin; the world tells us to enjoy everything that brings us pleasure without any thought of responsibility for our actions. God tells us to proclaim His promises by faith and walk towards their fulfilment; the world tells us to only believe what we see and stay grounded in our many fears. God tells us to give; the world tells us to keep. God tells us to love and forgive; the world tells us to hate and get even.

Whatever God says, the world's system is programmed for the exact opposite.

Jesus told us that we were to live by the words that came from His Father. He lived by them and overcame death, hell and the grave. Our testimony can be the same, if we resolve to do and say all that is written:

> *But He answered and said, 'It is written, "Man shall not live by bread alone, but by every word that proceeds from the mouth of God".' (Matthew 4:4)*

Do you want your words to produce what is good and peaceful in your life? Then you must know which words are God's words that produce faith, and which words are the devil's words that produce fear. Then you must speak out God's words so that the Holy Spirit can establish in your heart the realities that those words express.

As your heart changes, out of that transformed heart will come new faith-filled words that will change your world.

> *Who is the man who desires life, and loves many days, that he may see good? Keep your tongue from evil, and your lips from speaking deceit. (Psalm 34: 12–13)*

WHAT YOU SAY, YOU SOW

Each of us are continually sowing seed into our lives by our words. But you can choose the seed you plant and the crop you harvest. Every farmer knows that seed produces after its own kind—if you plant wheat you won't get barley. So the seed you plant in your life is what you will produce.

If you choose to sow good things into your life by your words, your harvest will be good.

You can live a good, healthy, prosperous life or a bad, sick, poverty-stricken life. The choice is yours. The world teaches that control of our life is not in our hands, that we should just drift along and see what fate brings. But God says that the quality of our life invariably gets down to a single choice which He has given us:

> *I have set before you life and death, blessing and cursing; therefore choose life, that both you and your descendants may live. (Deuteronomy 30:19)*

The best seed to plant is not our own words but the Word of God. By saying what God says about us, we guarantee we are always speaking the truth. God tells us to constantly think on things which will reproduce the qualities of His life in us:

> *Finally, brethren, whatever things are true ... noble ... just ... pure ... lovely ... of good report ... any virtue ... anything praiseworthy—meditate on these things. (Philippians 4:8)*

What words will you live by? Will you say what God says about you? Or what the devil says? God sees you as His valuable and precious child, free to be in perfect health, have abundant prosperity and enjoy peace of mind. The devil sees you as his sworn enemy, sick, tired, defeated, depressed and poor. He has one aim: to keep you that way for as long as you live.

I would rather die and go home saying what God says about me than surrender my words to the voice of unbelief and fear that's in the world.

> *My son, give attention to my words . . . keep them in the midst of your heart; for they are life to those who find them, and health to all their flesh.* (Proverbs 4: 20–24)

You can decide now to be a winner in life going somewhere to happen—not a loser wondering just what is happening!

Chapter 2

How Words Affect You

Death and life are in the power of the tongue, and those who love it will eat its fruit.
(Proverbs 18:21)

I discovered very early in life how profound the effect of words can be. I carried seeds of rejection right from the womb, for my birth was often referred to as a 'mistake'. Hearing these words spoken to me and about me were painful and did little to help me develop a healthy self-image and confidence.

As a girl I played tennis with home-made clothes and a hand-me-down racquet because we couldn't afford new ones. Somehow this made me more determined to succeed, but I had to continually work myself up to believe I could achieve my aims. I knew I had the ability, but I did not have the confidence.

My mum never wanted me to play tennis at all. She always encouraged me to quit the game despite my talent. All the time she felt something bad was going to happen to me because I was so far away. She thought I was on every plane that crashed, regardless of where I was in the world at the time! Because of my mum's fears, I grew up thinking care and worry were normal responses to life. Many of her anxieties carried over to me.

Thankfully, my dad was not so negative. When my tennis talent emerged to show I had a future among the world's top players, he encouraged me by constantly telling me he thought I was the best. His words helped inject a small amount of confidence into me. It was a comfort to know he believed in my dream to be the first Australian woman to win Wimbledon.

I was also blessed to have coaches who believed I could do it and told me so all the time. Often during match play I was tempted to quit, but I never did because I could actually 'see' and 'hear' their words in my mind. I would lift my game to meet their expectations, mostly with 100 per cent results. Because I had such poor self-esteem, it was very important to me not to disappoint the people who really believed in me. Their confidence gave me confidence.

Year after year my belief in my ability slowly grew. But it was a hard battle.

Apart from grappling with fears from words spoken over me as a child, I had another barrier to overcome to win Wimbledon: the negative press. I found out very early that journalists are not there to write the positives but to look for the negatives.

After my inexplicable 1961 loss as the number one seed in the first round, they saw my nerves as my Achilles heel and proceeded to exploit this fact on every possible occasion. There was no way they were going to let me forget my mistakes. Every year they turned up in full force to see whether the 'Aussie Amazon' could finally overcome her centre court jitters and take home the coveted trophy. Headlines screamed from the sporting pages, CAN SMITH EVER WIN WIMBLEDON?, effectively destroying the small amount of confidence I had developed from winning every other Grand Slam title in the world. Sometimes, when I went out in ordinary clothes and no one recognised me, I would hear people talking about me, not realising I was standing in front of them. Comments such as 'I don't like the way she plays' or 'She'll never win' were not the words I needed to hear.

Every year I came in as the No. 1, fit, strong and well-prepared, just as I was for every tournament. Yet Wimbledon always remained my bogey tournament. The difference was not in the physical preparation but in the mental arena. I tried desperately to put all the negative words from my mind. To win I had to believe 100 per cent that I could do it. But I knew there was that small area of fear, placed there by those negative words, lying just beneath the surface of my outward composure. This fear worked against me in the final matches I should have won.

Had I known then what I know today about the power of words, I would have won six Wimbledons, not just three!

I never had a problem with any tournament in the world except Wimbledon, because no other press in the world was as savage as the British press. The American press was lavish in praise for good performances and always looked for the positives in my game. Perhaps this helped me win my five US Opens, for what they wrote I tended to perform.

WHAT WE TELL OURSELVES

All of us have a story to tell of words and their effect on our lives. If we are asked to remember the most hurtful or lovely words ever spoken to us or about us, we can easily bring them to mind.

All of us have a story to tell of words and their effect on our lives.

Tragically, some people never rise above the limitations put on them by other people's words—the repeated put-downs of parents, the snide teasing of school friends, the supposedly 'prophetic' words that come from psychics, mediums and others who deal with familiar spirits.

While what others say about us is powerful, even more powerful is what we say about ourselves. It wasn't just the negative words of the press that caused me such problems at Wimbledon. It was the fact that too often I secretly echoed those words myself.

If we are told often enough that we are useless, hopeless or stupid we will eventually say the same things about ourselves.

If we are told often enough that we are useless, hopeless, stupid or good for nothing we will eventually start to say the same things about ourselves. The more we say, the more we will believe those soul-destroying words. And when we believe them, we will fulfil them to the letter.

I was always saying how scared, timid, shy and nervous I was about everything except my tennis game. Give me a tennis racquet and ball and I was confident and full of faith. Put me in front of a group of Rotarians who wanted me to speak about my achievements and I would be a total wreck. 'Forget it', I would say to my husband Barry, who encouraged me to accept some speaking engagements. I was a mess for three days before a talk, and by the time I got there I had broken out in a red rash. I always tried to make an excuse not to go.

Positive words had built faith into me in one area only, my tennis. But in every other area I was fragile, shaky and scared. My fears had such a strong hold over me I did not even realise they were controlling my life. Even in tennis my battlefield was often not the court but my own mind. When I believed I could win and said as much, I usually did. But when I believed I couldn't and said as much, I always lost. We say such bad things about ourselves: 'I'm ugly', 'I'm dumb', 'I'm lonely', 'I'm sick', 'I'm depressed', 'I'm a failure', 'My hair is always a mess'. Instead we should say: 'I'm beautiful', 'I'm lovely', 'I'm successful', 'I'm a winner', 'I'm smart', 'I'm righteous', 'I'm healthy', 'I'm happy'—all the things that God says we are. For God created us, and He doesn't make junk!

WORDS THAT CAUSE REJECTION AND REBELLION

The words that come out of our mouths today are often those we heard during our early lives. From my

The words that come out of our mouths today are often those we heard during our early lives.

years of ministry experience I can say that few of us have had a loving, caring, positive upbringing that fostered healthy self-esteem and a good self-image. As a result, our words for the most part reflect the rejection, fear, negativity and lack of love we were exposed to in those years.

Once we could understand the words being spoken to us, our wonderful world of believing we could do anything was shattered. From the time we were born our world was created by lots of don'ts and very few do's. If we went outside at night, we were told, the boogeyman would get us. If we tried to climb a fence or gate we were sure to fall and break our necks. If we went swimming too soon after lunch we would drown. If we crossed the road without looking we would be as dead as a door nail.

Childhood for many of us was a world of fear, and eventually that fear took over the faith we once had. What is true of fear is also true of other things that imprison us—rejection, for example. The rejection I suffered when it became clear to me that my parents hadn't wanted me born certainly left its mark.

Rejection always causes rebellion, and at school I found it hard to accept the authority of my teachers. One day I simply walked out and never returned. Later I was labelled 'rebel with a cause' for standing against the Australian Lawn Tennis Association over a decision that was blatantly against the interests of the touring players at the time. The cause was nobler, but there was still that rebellious streak in me flowing from the rejection in my life.

Rebellion is a trait that characterised the devil's stand against God and earned him rejection from the very throne-room of God. Rebellion that flows from rejection always leads to more rejection. Rebellious children are rejected, for few people like to have unruly children in their homes. Workers who are not loyal to their set tasks will be rejected. Husbands or wives who will not love each other unconditionally will eventually suffer rejection. Young people who rebel against society's laws will be rejected. The world has rejected and always will reject those who are rebellious.

But God will never reject any who come to Him. God can reach in and touch wounded hearts. Being accepted with open arms by God into His family leads to the banishment of rejection and rebellion, as I discovered personally.

The Destructive Power of Lying

Lying is another way we can dig ourselves into a deadly pit with our words. Deception from our mouths can destroy both our reputation and our relationships.

A man's word was once his bond, but now words are cheap and verbal contracts are rarely made. A handshake was once considered a binding oath, and men would give their lives rather than sacrifice the integrity of their solemn word. But today, even court room oaths taken on the Bible are no real hindrance to those who decide to speak dishonestly.

When we lie, others may believe our words, but we can't deceive ourselves. Twisted or perverse speech is speaking against the truth, and there is an awesome price to pay for this transgression: '*The truthful lip shall be established forever, but a lying tongue is but for a moment*' (Proverbs 12:19). In Proverbs 6:16–19, God lists 'a lying tongue' as one of seven 'abominations' He hates. He knows the destructive power of a lie, both to the person who is told the lie and the person who tells it.

The most serious consequence of lying is that those who live in deception find they are unable to trust the words of God because deceit rules their heart. When we can't trust what comes out of our mouths, we certainly can't trust the words that have come out of God's mouth and have been faithfully recorded in the Bible. Nor can we trust God's words when we speak them. As we shall see in chapter 4, if you can't believe in what you say, you will find that when you speak God's words you will doubt those too.

God tells us that all of our words should be honest, true and dependable, just as His are:

> *That which has gone from your lips you shall keep and perform, for you voluntarily vowed to the Lord your God what you have promised with your mouth. (Deuteronomy 23:23)*

> *Nor shall you swear by your head, because you cannot make one hair white or black. But let your 'Yes' be*

'Yes,' and your 'No,' 'No'. For whatever is more than these is from the evil one. (Matthew 5:36–37)

Honesty and integrity actually increase the power of our words. They ensure that the things we say can always be trusted.

THE LIBERATING POWER OF GOD'S WORD

If we constantly use our mouths to gossip, wound, hurt, criticise and judge others, we reveal something about ourselves. These type of words spring from hearts that have been hurt, wounded and rejected. But if we use our mouths to speak the Word of God—all that is true, noble, just, pure, lovely, of good report, virtuous and praiseworthy—we will find that this Word penetrates deep into our spirit, healing and restoring us.

God has not left us to flounder among the damage that words cause. Here are four steps to begin experiencing the liberating power of His Word.

1. Learn the true power of words. Our first task is to truly comprehend the awesome power of our words. God's Word says repeatedly that we *will* have what we say.

This principle can't be changed. People may violate godly principles but they can never alter them. A man may jump from a tall building in the belief that he can change the law of gravity, but he will quickly find he can't. He can try to break the law, but in so doing the law will break him.

In the same way, we may believe we can successfully violate God's laws, but we will soon find we can't. The spiritual principle that we reap what we sow with our words will always hold true.

2. Let go of the negativity of the past. Poor experiences in the past may have framed your words, but you can change all that with just one godly decision. You can let go of the past and learn to change its negativity through the Word of God.

The circumstances of your childhood may have greatly affected you, but you can't live in the past. You must press on. If you don't, you will have a poor future—always looking back over your shoulder (with its huge chip) to find someone or something else to blame for where you are today.

What happened to you may have been unfortunate or even tragic, but you can't afford to spend one more day in the world of 'if only'. It's time to give it all to God. He is the only one who can restore your situation. (I'll say more about leaving the past behind in chapter 8.)

3. Guard against evil words. We can be made instantly happy or depressed by what we see and hear. Our eyes and ears are the gateways to our mind, just as our mind is the gateway to our spirit.

If evil words gain access to our lives, they condemn us to a destiny far below God's best.

The book of Proverbs talks about guarding our hearts against evil words. If they gain access to our lives they condemn us to a destiny far below God's best.

Keep your heart with all diligence, for out of it spring the issues of life. (Proverbs 4:23)

The evening television news is a prime example of the world's negativity. The media are not interested in showing any good news; instead they give us everything that is speculative, dishonest, unjust, depressing and tragic. With satellite and cable television we can now take in bulletins of gloom and doom at all hours of the day and night. After we have watched them, we feel like someone has backed up a truck and dumped the whole weight of the world's problems on our shoulders.

If we let those stories, complete with their graphic pictures, get down into our hearts, we can go to bed full of grief, depression, sickness and despair—and all because of things that before we switched on the news were not even in our minds!

Instead, we should listen to words which build us up and encourage us. First and foremost among these are God's words. God's Word will never create an image of defeat or negativity. If the devil can get us to take his words of fear we will surely fail, but if we take God's words and keep our eyes and ears fixed on them, we will surely win.

God's Word will never create an image of defeat or negativity.

4. Say what God says. Instead of speaking the negatives of our lives, we need to start saying how big and powerful our God is. We need to praise God for His goodness and kindness, for the Word of God does not *ever* return to Him devoid of power:

So shall My word be that goes forth from My mouth; it shall not return to Me void [empty of power to fulfil], but it shall accomplish what I please, and it shall prosper in the thing for which I sent it. (Isaiah 55:11)

If we want our circumstances to change we need to stop voicing our fears, concerns and worries, even though they may be a very real issue in our lives. We can't live above the words we speak about ourselves or others, so we need to speak the highest words possible—the words of God. When we take our eyes off our circumstances and put them onto God's words, we will speak faith, not fear.

When we take our eyes off our circumstances and put them onto God's words, we will speak faith, not fear.

WORDS OF TRUTH

The first word of God some people need to know and speak is that God truly loves them. It's amazing how few people really believe that God loves them just as much as He loves Jesus. Every single person is precious to God.

You can personalise God's Word this way:

But God demonstrates His own love toward me, in that while I was still a sinner, Christ died for me. (Romans 5:8)

> *For I am persuaded that neither death nor life, nor angels nor principalities nor powers, nor things present nor things to come, nor height nor depth, nor any other created thing, shall be able to separate me from the love of God which is in Christ Jesus my Lord. (Romans 8:38–39)*

> *Behold what manner of love the Father has bestowed on me, that I should be called a child of God! (1 John 3:1)*

There are many areas where we need to counter negativity with God's words of truth. The world says, for example, that we all have to be sick sometime. But God's Word says, *'by His [Jesus'] stripes we are healed'* (Isaiah 53:5), and we can walk in health all the days of our life. Dying can be as simple as sitting down and committing our spirit into the hands of our Father God, just as Jesus did from the Cross. It's possible to die in perfect health at a fine old age.

Or again, the world says that we should be poor if we are true Christians. God's Word says that we are prosperous and that the world's wealth is laid up for us:

> *... the wealth of the sinner is stored up for the righteous. (Proverbs 13:22)*

Those who have a poverty mentality need to remind themselves that Jesus had a ministry group of twelve men on the road, and the finances generated obviously warranted the services of a treasurer, Judas.

It is this sort of truth that we need to find and speak out. And Jesus said that knowing the truth would make us free.

SPEAKING OF THINGS THAT ARE NOT

In John 17:17 Jesus prays to His Father, *'Sanctify them by Your truth. Your word is truth'*. The word 'sanctify' means 'to set apart' or 'separate from'. This means that when we hear the truth about salvation we can be set apart from eternal death. When we hear the truth about healing we can be set apart from sickness, disease and depression. When we hear the truth about prosperity we can be set apart from lives of poverty. When we hear the truth about peace, we can be set apart from lack of peace. You may look at your life and say these things are not there. But one of the things I love about God is that He likes to speak of things that *are not* as if they *are*, so that they will become what He calls them!

Nowhere is this better seen than when God sends an angel to His man Gideon.

The angel's greeting was not exactly what you would expect an angel to give someone hiding in fear from his enemies, as Gideon was: *'The Lord is with you, you mighty man of valour!'* (Judges 6:12). But God sent those words for a reason. He wanted to change the image Gideon had of certain defeat and impending death into one of victory and life.

It worked. Gideon was strengthened for the battle ahead, and we watch in amazement as he rises to the level of those prophetic words and defeats the enemy, even though he is greatly outnumbered.

God called Gideon something he was not, and Gideon changed to become what God called him.

We too can turn our lives around by speaking of 'things that are not' as if they are. Alternatively, we can also speak of things that are (fear, rejection, negativity, defeat) as if they are not. So many of us are busy saying the 'things that are' and we get exactly what we say. God tells us to say what we *desire*, not what we *have*, for we will have what we say:

We can turn our lives around by speaking of 'things that are not' as if they are.

So Jesus answered and said to them, 'Have faith in God. For assuredly, I say to you, whoever says *to this mountain, "Be removed and be cast into the sea," and does not doubt in his heart, but believes that those things he* says *will be done, he will have whatever he* says.' *(Mark 11:22–23)*

CHAPTER 3
GOD'S WORDS

Heaven and earth will pass away, but My words will by no means pass away.
(Matthew 24:35)

The 18th century humanist philosopher Voltaire once said that the Bible was archaic, outdated and would go out of vogue in his lifetime. His lifetime has well gone, but the Bible is still the world's largest selling book. Ironically, his former house in Paris now houses an office of the International Bible Society.

Voltaire would have done well to heed what God says about His Word never passing away and to have paid more attention to his own imminent passing away!

Unfortunately, Voltaire's opinion is rife in the world today. When God's Word is ridiculed or ignored, society experiences great periods of darkness and distress. Crime becomes rampant as authorities throw up their hands in despair, not realising that ignorance of God's Word is the reason behind people's descent into greater and greater levels of sin.

No political agenda or program of social reform has ever solved the sin problem, or ever will. Only Jesus, the living Word of God, can solve this disease of the human heart.

When God's Word is ignored, human life is no longer valued. Today the plight of an endangered species or a beached whale has multitudes volunteering their services and donating their money. But the same people who will stand in freezing water all night long to nurse a stricken mammal are unwilling to help a drunk in the gutter or a drug addict dying in the street.

When God's Word is ignored, human life is no longer valued.

Human life has become cheap. The planned efforts of the abortionist to end life before it begins are matched by the efforts of supporters of euthanasia to end it before it is really over. Abortion, perhaps more than any other issue, reveals the hedonistic tendency of human beings to enjoy their actions without thought of the outcome. God abhors the taking of life, for He is the author of life.

If the world is a mess today it is because the church has failed to hold to God's Word and preach the true gospel, which will always liberate people from the curse inherent in the fall of man. There are very few people in our generation who know the liberating truth of God's Word. Even those who profess to be religious are often ignorant of the truth of the Scriptures. They blindly follow the traditions of their

There are very few people in our generation who know the liberating truth of God's Word.

particular denomination without really knowing if their doctrines and practices line up with the Word of God.

Jesus rebuked such people in His own day, the learned scribes and Pharisees: *'You are mistaken, not knowing the Scriptures nor the power of God'* (Matthew 22:29).

Under Jesus' ministry, people were truly set free from the bondage placed on them through the Law. They saw the power of God expressed in His life because He knew God's Word and allowed the Holy Spirit to destroy their burdens.

Jesus lived by the Word and the Spirit, and His life was filled with freedom and power. God wants every one of us to live the same way. The key is in the power of the Word that we confess.

GOD'S WORD IS . . .

God's Word is the most powerful force in the universe. This is because God and His Word are one. They cannot be separated. And God is always watching over His Word to fulfil it.

God and His Word are one.

God's Word is *true*. His Word is His bond. His words are eternal and unchangeable because they are settled forever in heaven through the shedding of Jesus' blood on Calvary. When we speak God's Word into our earthly situations, we are saying that things here on earth are to be the same as they are in heaven.

God's Word is *holy* and *pure*. I used to wonder what it was that was 'pure' when I read in Philippians 4 that I was to keep my mind on things that were true, noble, just and pure. Then I discovered that God's Word is pure: *'Every word of God is pure'* (Proverbs 30:5).

God's Word is *eternal*. God has never withdrawn the power of His words from the earth, nor will He. For His Word is eternal, just as He is. God's Word is the only restraint on evil and the only way that evil can be changed. God has given us His Word as our 'TV guide' to life.

God has never withdrawn the power of His words from the earth.

God's Word has *power*. It has the power to change situations and transform lives. It has the power to bring people to salvation, to loose them from the bondages and addictions of the world, to heal everyone who is sick in mind or body.

He sent His word and healed them, and delivered them from their destructions. (Psalm 107:20)

God's Word coming out of the mouth of a believer is just as powerful as when it came out of the mouth of the living Word, Jesus!

THE MAKER'S INSTRUCTION BOOK

The Bible does not contain God's Word; it *is* God's Word. Every word in the Bible is God-breathed:

All Scripture is given by inspiration of God, and is profitable for doctrine, for reproof, for correction, for instruction in righteousness. (2 Timothy 3:16)

God's Word is full of golden nuggets of wisdom. Gold prospectors have found that the richest veins of ore are buried deep in the earth and require time, energy and expense to remove. Likewise, God's Word is available to all, but it takes time, energy and some expense to dig out the treasure. Desire and diligence on our part are needed to extract that wisdom and apply it to our lives.

Most homes have a Bible, but very few of us know what is written in it. In my early Christian life I did not even know the basic instruction that we are to read, study and memorise the Scriptures as surely as we take our daily food. Instead, I was dining on a diet of religious pomp, ceremony and tradition, a menu which always undermines the Word of God.

When I began to understand the power of God's Word it revolutionised my life. I discovered that the Bible is the source of all spiritual knowledge. It's our manual for life, our instruction book. When we live by its precepts, we will live a godly life to our full potential and purpose.

The Bible is the source of all spiritual knowledge.

If we buy a new video player and don't follow the manufacturer's instructions closely, we will never get the maximum benefit from our purchase. In the same way, we can't expect success in life if we don't follow our Maker's instructions. We neglect them at our peril.

Blowing the Devil's Disguise

The devil, of course, will do whatever he can to make us ignore God's Word. He attacks the Bible like nothing else.

He knows all too well that his chances of populating hell are greatly diminished when people find out the truth about God—and about the devil himself. He is content to hide behind his caricature as the dude in red pyjamas carrying a three-pronged pitch fork. No one could possibly believe in that! People's ignorance of Satan is his greatest weapon in deceiving them into tasting the tree of evil under the illusion that there is no price to pay.

Satan has many ways of attacking God's Word. For a long time he made sure the Bible was taken out of the hands of the common person and controlled by the clergy, the majority of whom greatly abused their position as custodians of God's words. They hid the liberating truth of the true gospel to advantage themselves. Instead of teaching God's Word as it is written, they preached their own man-made traditions and enslaved men and women in religious bondage.

These were truly the Dark Ages. They only lifted when great reformers like Martin Luther brought the truth of God's Word back into the earth.

Today Satan still attacks the Bible through the very ones who should be defending it. The church has so often compromised God's Word to accommodate political power, situational ethics, human ideas and hedonistic pleasures. God's Word never changes to meet any situation; it remains the same yesterday, today and forever. The body of Christ worldwide needs to stand up and say what God says about the issues that confront the modern world.

God's Word never changes to meet any situation.

It is no wonder Satan hates the Bible. God's Word is the way He has given us to overcome the forces of evil. We see this clearly in the ministry of Jesus, who was able to defeat the devil time and time again by saying, *'It is written'*. The devil could not stand against what God had decreed.

If we take God's Word into our lives and begin to speak and act it, it will be a barrier to the devil's plans of destruction. God has given us His Word to protect us from the devil, who cannot rob, kill or destroy us if we stay under the protection of the Word. When Israel obeyed God's commands, they came out of Egypt with no one sick and everyone prospering. When we obey His Word and walk in faith and love, we too will walk in His great blessings.

WHERE TO FIND GOD

We find God in His Word. There is only one God for all people for all time, not a myriad of gods for different nations. Philosophies abound that teach

God is not a real spiritual being, but is whatever the individual perceives him, her or it to be. This theme permeates modern thought, for the devil has done a good job in convincing the world that Christian intolerance of any other way than Jesus is a contradiction of the very Beatitudes taught by Him.

The idea that all roads lead to God sounds idealistic, but it is not truth. There are absolutes. God is spirit, a three-in-one being, Father, Son and Holy Spirit, with Jesus taking on human form to give the godhead expression in the world. God is not an aura, a cosmic consciousness or a figment of a fertile imagination. And Jesus died for the *whole* world. As He said, *'I am the way, the truth, and the life. No one comes to the Father except through me'* (John 14:6).

Many people embrace New Age practices and Eastern mysticism in an attempt to find the spiritual reality missing in their lives. They know they have not found it previously in religious practices centred around human traditions, rituals and ceremonies. But chanting meaningless OMs is not the way to find God either. He is found in His written Word.

In God's Word you find the realities of the spirit, for God is spirit and His Word is spirit.

God's Word Is Conceived In Us by His Spirit

I said earlier that we need to read our Maker's instruction book, just as someone needs to read the manual of a new video player to make it work. I recently purchased a new video player. But the sad truth is, even if I do read the manual, I know I will be none the wiser. I'm ignorant of most technical procedures. I need someone to explain it to me.

This is the way it is with the Bible. We have been given the wonderful gift of life, and with it our Maker's guidelines on how to maintain and live that life successfully and productively. But some who read the guidelines find them too hard to understand, and throw them aside instead of seeking help.

I have often found other people very helpful in my attempts to understand what God's Word is saying. But the most important help comes from God Himself, who has sent His Spirit to lead us into all truth (John 16:13).

The Holy Spirit wonderfully illuminates the Word of God to us. Jesus, the living Word, was conceived by the Holy Spirit. And the Word of God is also conceived in *our* spirit by the Holy Spirit.

The Holy Spirit wonderfully illuminates the Word of God to us.

Before we were born again of the Spirit of God, we were totally dominated by our body and mind, which were conformed to the negative ways of the world. Change only comes when the eyes of our understanding are opened to the truth of the gospel. This is the wonderful ministry of the Holy Spirit, who brings illumination to our minds and conviction to our hearts by revealing the truth of the Scriptures.

How I Discovered the Power of God's Word

In the early years of my Christian life, I did not know how to ask the Holy Spirit to reveal the truth of the Word to me. I received a lot of spiritual-type healing ministry, but it was all based on emotions with little emphasis on the Word.

So I had no real stability in my life. I only felt good when I felt good—I was totally dominated by my see-sawing emotions. One day I was happy, the next miserable.

I had no idea of the importance of God's Word in the development of faith, nor of the principle that '*faith comes by hearing, and hearing by the word of God*' (Romans 10:17). There was no growth in me. I suffered defeat after defeat. Though I was only thirty-nine, I felt like I had the body of an eighty year old. Poor health and the pressure of trying to handle four young children had a terrible effect on me. The fear that I was not coping just added to my long list of worries. I ended up on three different types of medication, one for a torn heart valve, one for depression and one for insomnia.

The problem was that I was *not* hearing the Word of God. Consequently my spirit could not receive it and grow in faith. All the rejection, hurt, bitterness and unforgiveness in my life made it worse. I did not know how to beat these unwelcome emotions.

Since I had no faith to overcome these areas of defeat, I almost gave in to them and very nearly lost my sanity and my life. Forget 'living in victory'—I was doing well just to drag my tired, weary body around the house, trying to be a good wife and mother. I kept thinking I had things a lot better out there on the tennis circuit before I became a Christian. I knew there had to be more to life than constantly popping pills and being so depressed I didn't want to go on living.

It was only after some faith-filled men came to me and led me in the direction to hear God's Word about healing that I started to recover. Every day I read the Word and found the specific Scriptures relating to healing. I spoke those words, personalising them by making the 'you's' in the Bible say 'me'. At first I did not truly believe them, but I kept on anyway. I wanted revelation of them down in my heart.

One key Scripture was Philippians 4:13, *'I can do all things through Christ who strengthens me'*. Every day I kept saying hundreds of times, over and over again, 'I can do all things through Christ who strengthens me. I can do all things through Christ who strengthens me'. I still felt like I had the body of an eighty year old. But now I sensed I was on the road to recovery, even though it did not look like it.

I knew to stay with the Word of God. One thing I had learned through tennis was that if I wanted to win, I had to stay in the game. Even when it looked like I was down and out, I never gave in until the final ball was played and the result beyond doubt. Winners are not quitters.

The Word finally 'became flesh' to me one day

when a dear friend, Helen, came to my home. She said she thought I looked dreadfully tired. Immediately I turned and said, 'No! I can do all things through Christ who strengthens me!'—and at that moment the power of God hit me. I felt instantly different. It was as if I had been plugged into a light socket and volts of electricity were shooting through me. I went down onto the court the next day and felt like I did when I was eighteen. I had been truly refreshed and strengthened, just as God promised:

> *Those who wait on the Lord shall renew their strength; they shall mount up with wings like eagles, they shall run and not be weary, they shall walk and not faint. (Isaiah 40:31)*

There was a supernatural force of faith flowing out from me. The Word had conceived in me and brought forth healing.

The Holy Spirit had been working with me in a powerful way. He had taken the Word that I had diligently placed into my spirit and had painted a wonderful image of being sound in mind and body on the canvas of my heart. Finally, once I truly believed what I was speaking, He had been able to act on the words I had spoken in faith and bring the miracle of my healing to pass. For *'faith comes by hearing, and hearing by the word of God'*.

All the doubt, fear and unbelief had left, and my days of sickness and defeat were over. I had always hoped that this would happen. I had long prayed that

God would heal me or take me home. But until I applied God's Word and acted on it in faith, I never received an answer.

God is listening for His Word to come out of our mouths so He can act on it and bring it to pass in our lives. The devil is also listening for *his* words to come out of our mouths, so he can bring *his* words to pass. Our choice of words gives God or the devil permission to work.

God is listening for His Word to come out of our mouths so He can act on it in our lives.

God fulfils His Word when He hears us speaking it out in faith.

> *So shall My word be that goes forth from My mouth; it shall not return to Me void [empty of power to fulfil], but it shall accomplish what I please, and it shall prosper in the thing for which I sent it. (Isaiah 55:11)*

CHAPTER 4
WORDS OF FAITH

Faith comes by hearing, and hearing by the word of God.
(Romans 10:17)

Every person who is born again of the Spirit of God has faith already. *'God has dealt to each one a measure of faith'*, says Paul (Romans 12:3). If you are a believer, faith is not something you can have or not have; you have it!

No one can pray to be given faith, nor is it right for any Christian to say they don't have faith. Every person has been given a measure of faith, and no one receives a greater measure than another.

The day we accept Jesus Christ as our Lord and Saviour is the day that God deposits His kind of faith in our spirit. This faith is a spiritual force that enables us to accomplish the seemingly impossible and overcome every conceivable adversity.

When we accept Jesus as Lord and Saviour, God deposits His kind of faith in our spirit.

For whatever is born of God overcomes the world. And this is the victory that has overcome the world—our faith. (1 John 5:4)

While each of us has a measure of faith, however, we can live in ignorance of what we have. People perish from lack of knowledge (Hosea 4:6), and Satan loves to keep us unaware that we have the God-kind of faith within us.

Every person is responsible for developing their measure of faith to its fullest. And all we have to do to develop it is to turn the switch of faith on—with our mouths.

When I was a young Christian I had a deep desire to know more about the things of God. Unfortunately, those to whom I turned for advice had little knowledge of the importance of the Word and even less knowledge of the God-kind of faith. But when I read the Bible I saw that *'without faith it is impossible to please Him'* (Hebrews 11:6), and without faith we can not live the way God designed us to live. Clearly, faith is essential for our walk here on earth.

But how could I get enough faith in my heart so that it choked out the fears of the world?

Gradually it dawned on me: since *'faith comes by hearing and hearing by the word of God'*, the equation was simple: no word, no faith!

THE WORD–FAITH EQUATION

Faith grows by hearing the Word of God constantly. The quickest way to grow in faith is to hear yourself saying the Word, meditating on it, muttering it, affirming it. Scriptural meditation is simply saying and thinking what God says. Like a cow chewing its cud, you go over it, meditate on it, think on it, speak it, again and again . . . until it gets down into your spirit and the Holy Spirit gives you a personal revelation of its truth.

The quickest way to grow in faith is to hear yourself saying the Word.

It's not enough to have a light snack of God's Word on a Sunday if we want to live in victory every day of the week. Nor can we pray for our faith to grow, for it is up to us to develop our spiritual 'faith muscle' by working out on God's Word every day. There are no short cuts. A low 'word level' means a low 'faith level'.

It is up to us to develop our 'faith muscle' by working out on God's Word every day.

It is news to many people that hearing the Word of God is the way to grow spiritually and increase the force of their faith. Many of us have been taught that faith grows through tests and trials. I once thought this, until I realised that everything I was going through was not strengthening my faith at all. In fact, I was growing quite bitter and resentful against God. I thought that He could save me from my suffering but had chosen not to because of something I had done or not done that displeased Him.

To overcome this I had to learn to know my righteousness in Jesus—that nothing I could do or not do affected my status as God's child. I also had to learn how faith grows. Tests and trials don't increase our faith; they only *prove* it (or prove our fear). Faith comes not by adversity but by hearing.

It's no time to try to develop our faith when we are in the middle of a time of great testing. That's when we need to use the faith we already have. If we are constantly feeding ourselves faith when we don't need it, we will be able to release it when we do.

MOUNTAIN-MOVING FAITH

What is it like, this faith that God has placed in our hearts? Mark 11:23 tells us it's *mountain-moving faith*.

> *Whoever says to this mountain, 'Be removed and be cast into the sea,' and does not doubt in his heart, but believes that those things he says will be done, he will have whatever he says.*

Notice it's 'whatever he *says*' that is the key, not 'whatever he prays'.

What is the mountain in your life? Sickness? Depression? A difficult marriage? Financial hardship? Cancer? When you speak the Word of God in faith to that mountain, the Holy Spirit will act. All He is waiting for are your words.

God does not want us to put up with the mountains in our lives.

God doesn't want us to put up with the mountains in our lives. If you are sick in body, for example, don't let the mountain of sickness remain; speak to it and remind it that you are the temple of God and that it can't stay, for God's Word promises you redemption from the curse of sickness. You are not lying when you say what God says.

Keep speaking what God says about you. Keep the Word of God coming out of your mouth and going into your spirit. Faith is a force that flows out from the spirit and acts independently of the flesh and the mind. Since the Word of God is spirit, alive and living, it is exactly the food our spirit needs to grow the God kind of faith in us that will overcome the world.

BELIEVE WHAT *YOU* SAY

When God says we are to believe that the things we say will come to pass, it implies we must have faith in our words. It's one thing to talk about having faith in God's words, but faith in my own words . . . ? What does *that* mean?

When I was very sick I didn't believe in my words. I was speaking all the wrong things. I was hitting myself over the head, telling myself, 'I'm a worm. I'm nothing'. I didn't think God could use me—I had only heard how He used men out of the gutter, and I had been number one in the world. I had no belief in myself or what I said.

When I started to speak the Word of God for healing, I used to say, 'But Lord, I don't believe it. I doubt it in my heart'. Then I started to notice something. As I flooded myself with the Word, I did start to believe it in my heart. And then when I spoke it out, I found myself growing in trust in my words because they were God's words.

I used to have to say, 'Father, I believe that the things

which *I* say shall come to pass; I shall have whatever I say. I have faith in my words, because my words are alive, my words are living, my words are tangible and anointed because they are God's words. God and His Word are one, and I and my words are one.'

We frame our world with our words (Hebrews 11:3). We need to believe the words we speak before we can possibly believe the words God speaks.

HOW'S YOUR REPORT CARD?

Two men who believed in their own words because they were founded on God's Word were Joshua and Caleb. In Numbers 13 we read that they were among the twelve men sent out by Moses to spy out the Promised Land before the Israelites went in. After forty days in Canaan they returned.

Ten of the spies gave a wonderful account of a land flowing with milk and honey. Two men even carried back a huge cluster of grapes on a pole! But these men also said they had found strong enemies there, including giant men who made them feel like grasshoppers. On this basis, and forgetting the Word of God that had promised them victory, they changed their good report into an evil report, concluding that the Israelites were not able to go up and possess the land.

Joshua and Caleb, however, brought a good report, silencing the people before Moses, who had been distressed to find that the land could not be taken. Joshua and Caleb said, '*Let us go up at once and take possession, for we are well able to overcome it'* (Numbers 13:30).

An 'evil report' is simply one that contradicts God's Word. A 'good report' is one that believes what God says, despite the evidence of things in the natural realm that say the opposite.

Joshua and Caleb, according to God, were of a 'different spirit' to those who refused to believe (Numbers 14:24). They were totally convinced that what God had promised He would also perform. Like David when he faced Goliath and declared openly that his God would deliver the defiant Philistine into his hands (1 Samuel 17:47), Joshua and Caleb knew that the enemy awaiting them in the Promised Land would be delivered into their hands, for God had already said that the land was theirs. They just had to go forward in faith and trust God to fight the battles for them.

THE CONFESSION OF FAITH

A solid faith confession, in which we say what God says and not what our circumstances say, will always bring the desired victory. It may not be instant, but as the faith confession continues, the force of patience will grow to undergird our faith until the 'evil report' finally becomes the desired 'good report'. Joshua and Caleb never said anything contrary to their belief that Israel would possess the land. Due to the unbelief of their fellow Israelites they had to wait forty years, but they did finally receive according to what they believed. Their patience was tested, but they never changed their 'good report' to an 'evil report' simply because it looked as if it was not going to happen.

In Joshua 1:6–9 God told Joshua to *'be strong and of good courage'* and to be *'very courageous'*. To be courageous is to have the ability to meet danger without giving way to fear. Faith is the opposite of fear, and a large part of being courageous is to step out on God's Word alone and speak it in faith at all times, regardless of circumstances.

After forty years it was only those who agreed with God's Word who finally entered the Promised Land. Those who doubted His Word died in a wilderness of their own making, simply because they refused to believe, speak or act on the Word that God had given them.

And so it is in our lives. God has already spoken about our 'promised land'. The Bible shows how we can claim all the promises that are ours because of our wonderful new status as sons and daughters of God. He is not speaking anything new today, apart from greater revelation through His Spirit of what He has already spoken through His written Word. When our circumstances say something contrary to God's Word, we have to choose what we will believe—a 'good report' based on what God says, or an 'evil report' totally opposite to God's Word.

GOD'S 'GOOD REPORT'

God's 'good report' of our new life in Christ is found in the Bible. We are what the Word says we are, regardless of how we feel or think about it. Among other things:

• God's Word says we are righteous, therefore we *are* righteous—despite what we think about our unworthiness.

> *For He [God] made Him who knew no sin to be sin for us, that we might become the righteousness of God in Him. (2 Corinthians 5:21)*

• God's Word says we are forgiven, therefore we *are* forgiven—despite our feelings of guilt and self-condemnation.

> *There is therefore now no condemnation to those who are in Christ Jesus. (Romans 8:1)*

• God's Word says we are healed, therefore we *are* healed—despite what our bodies tell us to the contrary.

> *... by whose stripes [wounds] you were healed. (1 Peter 2:24)*

• God's Word says we are overcomers and have victory in our lives through our faith—even though we may look as though we are defeated.

> *For whatever is born of God overcomes the world. And this is the victory that has overcome the world—our faith. Who is he who overcomes the world, but he who believes that Jesus is the Son of God? (1 John 5:4–5)*

All this and much more describes who we are in Christ. *Whatever a believer in Jesus finds in the Word of God he can claim as being personally for him.* It's then up to him to take hold of it.

Someone could give us the title deed to a block of land that we have never seen, yet we know we have that land because we have the deed in our hand. And so it is with the Bible. The Word of God is our title deed to all that is rightfully ours, even though we may not be able to see it.

NOT 'NAME IT AND CLAIM IT'

I truly believe that our failure to confess God's Word from our mouths has time and time again stopped the power of our tongue creating what is good in our lives. Repeatedly we speak our fears, but few of us speak our faith.

Sophisticated theologies tell us that confession with our mouth is childish and foolish, so we keep our mouth firmly shut. And when we do speak, we are so engrossed in our fears, sins, guilt and emotions that we fail to confess faith.

We don't lie when we say about ourselves what God says about us.

To confess God's Word is not, as some claim, a 'name it and claim it' theology. It is, after all, *God's* Word that we speak. We don't lie when we say about ourselves what God says about us.

Yes, some people have 'named

and claimed' things, but not by speaking out in faith. It's in the motives of the heart. If your motives are not right—if you are not looking at Jesus—you will not receive anything anyhow. If your eyes are focussed on Jesus and you have the right heart attitude towards Him, He will bless you.

Some people ask why we need to speak God's Word aloud. Isn't it enough to think it in your mind? But God did not think the world into existence; He spoke it into existence! It's when the Word is *expressed* that it has creative power.

It is not enough to try to out-think our thoughts. We have to out-speak them.

When we speak God's Word aloud it strengthens our faith, for faith comes by hearing the Word. To speak aloud means we hear that word firsthand. We generally only speak what we believe, and what we believe is directly governed by what we hear:

> *Since we have the same spirit of faith, according to what is written, 'I believed and therefore I spoke,' we also believe and therefore speak.* (2 Corinthians 4:13)

Further, the mind is a battlefield of conflicting thoughts that gravitate somewhere between faith and fear the whole time. Faith and fear are complete opposites. Where there is faith there cannot be fear, and where there is fear there cannot be faith.

Faith will always bring about the desired positive result. It is so important to build faith into our thinking by hearing lots of God's Word. '*Faith comes by* hearing, *and hearing by the word of God*' (Romans 10:17).

FAITH WORKS!

I know faith works because it was by faith in God's Word that my own life was changed. It was by faith I was healed of heart disease, set free from depression and insomnia, and redeemed from fear. Victory only came when I took God at His Word and spoke and acted on that Word. I believed I was healed when everything in my mind and body said I was not. I had to learn to ignore the pain of my body and my depressed emotions and stand by faith for the healing which God's Word said was mine.

In other words, I chose to exalt the Word of God over my circumstances. Circumstances are temporary and subject to change. They are part of the 'seen' things which the Bible contrasts with the 'unseen':

> *For the things which are seen are temporary, but the things which are not seen are eternal. (2 Corinthians 4:18)*

As long as I diligently and faithfully applied the Word of God to my negative circumstances, they had to change. And eventually they did!

Spiritual things are more real than physical things. Any change in our lives must first take place in the spiritual realm before it will manifest in the natural realm. Faith is simply the connection between the natural realm and the spiritual realm. Faith brings the things the Word says from the realm of the supernatural (where they are already a reality) to the realm of the natural (where they need to become a reality).

Any change in our lives must take place first in the spiritual realm before it will manifest in the natural realm.

We need to think about, speak about and 'see' our answer before we have it. If we can't see it, we will never have it: *'Where there is no vision, the people will perish'* (Proverbs 29:18 KJV). If we are sick, for example, we need to see and speak ourselves into health through faith in God's Word, which says, *'by His stripes we are healed'* (Isaiah 53:5). By faith we bring the blessing from the spiritual realm into the natural realm.

The supernatural realm is like the wind: it can't be seen, but when it operates its effects are obvious. And faith is the same—invisible, but powerful in effect.

> *Faith is the substance of things hoped for, the evidence of things not seen. (Hebrews 11:1)*

CHAPTER 5
WORDS FOR THE HEART

My son, give attention to my words …
Keep them in the midst of your heart.
(Proverbs 4:20–21)

Recently I had some alarming symptoms in my body. I went to the doctor to find out what it was, so I could 'speak to the mountain' and tell it to go. The doctor said, 'You have a lump in your breast'. I was shocked.

I could not get in for tests for about three days, so I put myself away with the Word of God. Day and night I pushed into the Word, reading it, listening to tapes, and I cried out to the Lord as I had never cried out before.

In response, the Lord gave me a Scripture, Matthew 15:13: *'Every plant which My heavenly Father has not planted will be rooted up'*. My heavenly Father had certainly not planted this lump in my breast, so here was His promise to me that it would be uprooted from my body.

Mark 11:23 says to speak to the mountain and say, 'Be removed', so I started to say that about the lump in my breast. Night and day I repeated, 'Every plant which my heavenly Father has not planted in my body is rooted up and removed, in Jesus' name. Lump, you are uprooted, you don't live here any longer.' When I finally went for tests the technician said, 'I can't find anything'. The Word of God had focussed my faith and enabled my body to receive God's healing.

Matthew 15:13 was the particular Scripture I needed at that time, and God gave it to me. If we ask Him to show us, He will lead us to just the right words for our situation.

We can't take in the whole Bible at once. When I first entered Bible School in 1982 I was an absolute mess; I would walk into meetings and just want to cry. As God opened my eyes to His truth, one by one I found the Scriptures I needed to meet my needs. I began to write my needs down—heart condition, fear and so on—along with the Scriptures that God gave me to address each one. Then I started to say them. Within eight months the doctor gave me the news that my torn heart valve was totally healed. (I say more about how God dealt with my fear in chapter 9.)

God's Word must go deep into our spirit if it is to have any effect.

Mere head knowledge of the Bible is not enough. God's Word must go deep into our spirit if it's to have any effect. It must become God's Word *for me*. It must get into my heart.

A WORD FOR EVERY OCCASION

Nothing is impossible with God. If we speak His Word in faith, He can and will act on it. Our job is to find out the particular words that will strengthen our faith in each circumstance. There is a word of God for every single situation we face in the adversities of life. God has left no area uncovered.

There is a word of God for every situation we face in the adversities of life.

Many years ago, one of the ladies in my ministry team faced every mother's nightmare. Her baby son was abducted and taken out of the country. She had no idea where he was. Years of searching proved fruitless. Then she became a Christian, and God gave her a specific word:

> *Thus says the Lord: 'Refrain your voice from weeping, and your eyes from tears; for your work shall be rewarded, says the Lord, and they shall come back from the land of the enemy. There is hope in your future, says the Lord, that your children shall come back to their own border.' (Jeremiah 31:16–17)*

From that time on she knew she would one day see her son again and tell him she had never willingly given him up.

For twenty-five years she stood on this Scripture, constantly saying it and praising God for His promise to return her son 'to her border'. Then one day, after a miraculous search initiated by her adult son, he telephoned. He had become a Christian. Now they live in the same nation as a family once again and she is a proud and happy grandmother.

Never give up hope that God will turn your circumstances around.

(If your children have gone into the captivity of the enemy—whether it be drugs, alcohol, immoral living, homosexuality, crime or whatever—you must keep your faith strong and claim their full recovery. Your prayers should speak that deliverance over them all the time, for God's Word will certainly accomplish what all our worrying, crying and pleading cannot.)

DIGGING FOR GOLD

God wants us to grow in the knowledge of His Word, but this growth doesn't drop out of the sky. There is something we have to do. Proverbs 4:22 says God's words are *'life to those who find them'*. We have to *find* them.

If we want to find gold we have to go looking for it, as any prospector will tell you. It's the same with God's Word. Getting the Word is something we have to do ourselves. God doesn't prosper lazy people who cruise through life on the coat-tails of others.

Without the Word we remain spiritual babies.

Without the Word we remain spiritual babies. Babies are vulnerable to any adversary and easily destroyed. We may have sat in church all our lives, but if we don't know what God's Word says for ourselves, we are in fact babies and most deceived.

'Finding' the Word of God is not only a matter of discovering the words targeted to our need, but also of using them. Sometimes people take hold of the Word and say it once or twice, perhaps for a week or two, and then give up. Nothing seems to have happened. 'That Word doesn't work,' they say. They have failed to *find* it.

When I first started to learn about the power of my words, I used to think, 'Goodness! If I am what I am by the words of my mouth, how am I ever going to change my life around?' But it happened, one step at a time, as I learned to apply the Word of God.

For me it was like tennis. When I was playing under the great old coach Harry Hopman, he used to say to us, 'Hit for the lines'. In fact, that's all he ever said! He never told us anything else, never taught us anything about footwork or stroke-making. We simply got out on court for hours and did drills, just hitting for the lines, up and down the lines, cross court for the lines—the same thing over and over again.

That's what makes a champion. You put in the drills, the discipline, the work, and when you are in a match all the practice you have put in comes out.

We take in the Word of God in exactly the same way. Then, if we have spent the time putting it down into our spirit, when a situation arises in which it's needed it's there for us, bubbling up out of our heart.

WHERE THERE IS A NEED, PLANT A SEED

There is a great love and reverence returning for the Word of God in our day. More and more, people really do want to give attention to the Word for themselves. It's not enough to hear a Scripture once or twice. It must become our life.

The Word is like a seed. It must be planted deep where it can't be easily uprooted. Then it must be fed and watered. We do this by constantly going over it. It must be kept in the ground long enough for it to germinate, grow and bear good fruit. This takes time. But if we sow and nurture the seed, we shall reap the harvest.

The garden of our heart also needs to be protected from weeds of doubt, unbelief and fear. All these will try to choke the seed. The minute we choose to believe God's Word above our circumstances, the devil will rush us people—especially loving family members—who will try to convince us how foolish we are.

The garden of our heart needs to be protected from weeds of doubt, unbelief and fear. Faith is the only effective weedkiller.

Jesus showed us what to do with unbelievers when He went to Jairus' house to heal his daughter. He showed the door to those who would have inhibited the free flow of faith through their fear and unbelief (Mark 5:40). So must we if we are in a life and death situation.

In the end, our faith is the only effective weedkiller

on the spiritual market. We must strengthen it every day by a disciplined application of God's Word.

CHERISHING THE WORD

Sometimes people say the Bible is boring and too hard to understand. But when you get into the Word, you find your desire for it grows.

Giving attention to God's Word develops a desire for it in us.

Even in everyday life, devoting our time to something develops our desire for it. Hobbies, for example, which at first are pursued half-heartedly, can turn into pursuits that consume most of our time. I know this is what happened to me when I started to hit a tennis ball for fun. The more I played, the more I wanted to play, until it was all I wanted to do.

Giving attention to God's Word develops a desire for it in us.

The Scriptures are precious because they are God's love letters to us. We know how much we treasure words from a loved one and read and re-read every word they write to us. Eventually they are no longer mere words on a page; the wonderful image they create is etched on our minds and emotions.

When we read God's words, they too create an image in us—an image of ourselves as Jesus sees us, of the great love He has for each one of us, and of the indescribable future He has in store for us.

God's Word is infinitely more valuable to us than even the most cherished letters from a loved one. And just as we get to know those letters by heart, so too we should read God's Word until we know it by heart. It is said that when we hear we remember ten per cent; when we read we remember twenty-five per cent; when we study we remember seventy-five per cent; but when we memorise we remember 100 per cent.

THE MEDITATION OF OUR HEARTS

When God brings words to our notice, He expects us to go over them again and again until they are written on our hearts. We say them, repeat them, memorise them, declare them, picture them and meditate on them.

> *Let the words of my mouth and the meditation of my heart be acceptable in Your sight, O Lord, my strength and my Redeemer. (Psalm 19:14)*

True meditation is saying those words that will create a good picture in our minds and our hearts.

On our farming property, it's commonplace to see our cows chew their food over and over again. Once they have formed a 'cud', they swallow it and it is deposited in their stomach. After a time they bring it back up to chew over again, then drop this cud into their second stomach. This process is repeated several times.

This is the way we need to chew over God's Word.

One of the most helpful things I have found in meditating on the Word is to personalise it. Once again, I learned this when I was fighting fear. When I started to say the Scriptures aloud, I realised they needed to become real for me. They needed to become *part* of me. So over and over I would say, 'I haven't got a spirit of fear. God loves me and I love God. God has given me authority to trample on every power of the enemy. I have the mind of Christ and I can think like God. Greater is He who is within me than he who is in the world. I'm a victorious overcomer and can do all things through Christ who strengthens me.' I was putting myself in the Word.

The more I said these godly words, the more I believed them. Faith grew in me. As I heard myself speaking God's truth about myself, I became stronger and more confident that I was going to come through after all. It only took a few months before I was able to declare my complete and utter trust in God.

When we hear the Word of God it is like a healing balm to our minds and bodies.

When we hear the Word of God it's like a healing balm to our minds and bodies. Our minds can't go around and around in torment if we keep them centred on Jesus. We do this by keeping His Word before us day and night:

You will keep him in perfect peace, whose mind is stayed on You. (Isaiah 26:3)

Now that we have outlined the principles of speaking by faith, it's time to go on and see how they work in practice. We will start with the most basic topic of all: how we enter into the abundant life God has won for us in Jesus.

CHAPTER 6

HOW WORDS AFFECT YOUR DESTINY

I have come that they may have life, and that they may have it more abundantly.
(John 10:10)

Each of us has a God-given destiny to fulfil. We may fulfil certain goals and visions we have for ourselves, as I did in tennis—and indeed, God takes great delight when we accomplish things with the talents He has given us. I, for one, always knew that my talent was from God. But fulfilling our dreams is not the same as fulfilling our divine destiny.

Since God created us, He knows exactly what we need to live successful, peaceful and contented lives. We should all know who we are, where we come from and what we are going to do, as well as what we are *not* going to do. If we choose to live by what God says about these matters we will fulfil our God-given destiny. If we choose to live separated from Him, fulfilling our destiny will be impossible.

Since God created us, He knows exactly what we need to live successful, peaceful and contented lives.

A divine destiny is not one in which we walk when we go to heaven. God's words prepare us for living *this* life, not just the life hereafter! Our God-given destiny is to live a happy, contented, peaceful, loving, healthy and prosperous life now. This is the destiny God has planned for believers here on earth. Jesus walked in His destiny on earth (to redeem humankind) so that we can walk in our destiny on earth (to live an abundant life). Jesus could not fulfil this destiny in heaven any more than we can!

To know our divine destiny we must first know the God who made us. That's where we begin to enter into our destiny. And once again, it's tied up with our words.

I DISCOVER MY DESTINY

The only way to live a successful life here on earth is to live the way God wants us to live. If we live a natural life without any relation to God, we are destined to live a defeated life—even if we have all the trappings of fame and fortune.

I had it all. It was a great feeling to succeed in tennis and hold high the victor's crown on many wonderful occasions. But after the celebrations died down and the hard work began for the next tournament, I knew that my inner sense of emptiness had not gone away. The more I accomplished, the more I realised I was not going to find the peace I so desperately desired through any achievements on the tennis court.

The more I accomplished, the more I realised I was not going to find on the tennis court the peace I desperately desired.

My problem was separation from my Creator. Having been raised in a 'religious' environment, I knew all *about* God, but I did not know Him personally. There was an inner part of me that I knew only God could touch. Eventually I called out to Him as I sat in a majestic cathedral in Paris. I asked in a genuine, heartfelt manner to know Him better.

He did not disappoint me. Not long afterwards, back home in Perth on holidays, I was taken to a church meeting where I went forward to receive Jesus Christ as my Lord and Saviour. I knew people in that room recognised me because I was still the top-ranked player in the world. But I did not care. Pride was not going to stop me because I knew I needed God just as much as any person in that room.

No amount of money and none of the trappings of fame could have given me what I received that day. I stepped forward into a new life, proclaiming the promise of salvation God had given to all who will believe and speak:

> *If you confess with your mouth the Lord Jesus and believe in your heart that God has raised Him from the dead, you will be saved. For with the heart one believes to righteousness, and with the mouth confession is made to salvation.* (Romans 10:9–10)

I had never known that this prayer for salvation needed to be spoken. In fact, at this stage of my search for a more personal reality of God, I did not even know this prayer was in the Bible. I thought I would only be saved if I did enough good things on earth during my lifetime.

It was a revelation to me that this simple prayer, spoken sincerely from my heart, was enough to inherit the eternal life and salvation that I believed was only possible through going to church, keeping the sacrament and obeying the commandments. I discovered that day that even my belief in God would not have saved me, for even the devil believes there is a God—and that certainly will not save him (James 2:19)!

GRASPING SALVATION

By speaking out the beliefs of our heart and declaring them before God and the devil, we establish ourselves in the covenant promise of salvation. Just as men and women who wish to marry make binding verbal vows to each other in the presence of God and a number of witnesses, so we should stand and declare Jesus Christ before God and witnesses:

> *Whoever confesses Me before men, I will also confess before My Father in heaven. (Matthew 10:32)*

There are no words to describe the wonderful feelings of love, joy and peace that God gave me when I finally accepted His Son that day. My spirit came alive, and I knew a sense of well-being that I had never experienced before. I was alive to the things of God for the very first time, even though I had faithfully sat in a church pew for nearly thirty years. No one in all those years had told me that I needed to be 'born again':

> *Jesus answered and said to him, 'Most assuredly I say to you, unless one is born of water and the Spirit, he cannot enter into the kingdom of God. That which is born of the flesh is flesh, and that which is born of the Spirit is spirit. Do not marvel that I said to you, "You must be born again."' (John 3:5–7)*

I walked away from that meeting brimming over with the love and peace of God.

I went back on tour and told everyone that I had made Jesus my Lord. Not everyone wanted to hear, but I told them anyway. I was so in love with God. He had become real and personal to me in a way I never thought possible. I felt sorry for those around me who did not know Him as I had come to know Him.

I had left religion, with its legalistic set of rules, and embraced relationship.

I did not have a lot of knowledge at this point. But I sensed that I had left religion, with its legalistic set of rules and regulations to try and please God, and had embraced relationship, with a desire to serve God out of love, not duty. Now, like Adam before the Fall in the Garden, I knew I could come and talk to God any time, day or night. He was not some far-off figure but a close, loving and personal God who cared about me and everything I did.

Each of us needs a revelation of what Jesus really did for us. He brought us back into the place where we can walk and talk with God. We're God's children, sons and daughters of the Most High! When like me you receive Him as Lord, your divine destiny truly begins.

Keys to Destiny

Jesus is our example for living out our divine destiny. He knew where He came from and who He was. He knew what He could do. And He knew what He was *called* to do by His Father.

These are the keys to discovering our destiny. God wants us, too, to know who we are, what we can do and what we are called to do by Him.

God wants us to know who we are, what we can do and what we are called to do by Him.

Who we are. The world tells us that we are just a chance conglomeration of molecules assembled together, living a life of ups and downs and hoping that for the greater part we come out with more ups than downs. But God's Word tells us something wonderfully different. There we find that each of us is a unique, valuable and precious individual, created by God in the womb:

For You formed my inward parts; You covered me in my mother's womb. (Psalm 139:13)

The life of God was breathed into us at conception, just as God breathed His life into Adam in the original creation. We are so immensely precious to God that He sent His beloved Son, Jesus, to die for each one of us.

What we can do. As soon as we come into our new life as children of God we take our place as spiritual beings, already seated in heavenly places (Ephesians 1: 3–5). We are now able to operate in faith from a position of spiritual authority which enables us to overcome any adversity we face.

God guarantees we will live a truly successful, happy, peaceful and contented life through knowing Him. Jesus came to bring us a life far superior to any we could live if we followed the way of the world: '*I have come that they may have life, and that they may have it more abundantly*' (John 10:10).

What God calls us to do. God calls us to love Him with every fibre of our being:

You shall love the Lord your God with all your heart, with all your soul, and with all your strength. (Deuteronomy 6:5)

This is true worship. God created us to worship Him as part of our natural make-up. We are wired for worship.

If we don't worship God, we will invariably worship something or someone in His place. The thing on which we spend the greatest part of our time and money will show what we worship. It can be sport, business, possessions—or simply ourselves.

But ultimately, if God is not the object of our worship and living, we will have frustrating and disappointing lives, far below the best God has prepared for us.

WHAT IS OURS IN CHRIST

The basis for responding to what God *calls* us to do is to understand what we *can* do. In other words, we need to know what is ours in Christ. If we don't know what is ours then we can never claim it.

If we don't believe, for example, that we should be healed, we will never walk in divine health. If we don't know the peace of God which passes all understanding, we will never be able to say all is well with our souls. And so it is with every aspect of our life in Christ. If we don't know our full inheritance, if we don't appreciate what Jesus died to give us, then we will never walk in our divine destiny.

Imagine somebody gave you a million dollars, deposited it in an account in your name and gave you the account number. You could draw on that money any day, any time, and it would be yours. But if you did not know you had a million dollars, you would ignore the account and live in poverty.

Our faith will be no higher than our knowledge.

So it is with the Word of God. The Bible is our account book. We can draw on it any time. But we have to know what is in it. Our faith will be no higher than the knowledge we have.

GOD HAS GIVEN ALL WE NEED

In 2 Peter 1:1–8 the word 'knowledge' occurs five times:

> *Simon Peter, a bondservant and apostle of Jesus Christ, to those who have obtained like precious faith with us by the righteousness of our God and Saviour Jesus Christ: Grace and peace be multiplied to you in the* knowledge *of God and of Jesus our Lord, as His divine power has given to us all things that pertain to life and godliness, through the* knowledge *of Him who called us by glory and virtue, by which have been given to us exceedingly great and precious promises, that through these you may be partakers of the divine nature, having escaped the corruption that is in the world through lust. But also for this very reason, giving all diligence, add to your faith virtue, to virtue* knowledge, *to* knowledge *self-control, to self-control perseverance, to perseverance godliness, to godliness brotherly kindness, and to brotherly kindness love. For if these things are yours and abound, you will be neither barren nor unfruitful in the* knowledge *of our Lord Jesus Christ.*

Here we read that God has given us *'all things that pertain to life and godliness'*. In other words, we *already* have everything we need to live His abundant life. Wisdom, knowledge, grace, love, gentleness, meekness, temperance—you name it, we've got it!

And He has given us His *'exceedingly great and precious promises'*. All we have to do is *claim* and *proclaim* these promises by faith, and we will begin to see them working in our lives.

The devil, of course, doesn't want us to grow in the knowledge of what is rightfully ours. He wants to rob us of it before it gets down into our spirit and becomes heart-felt revelation to us. He wants to withhold what is rightfully ours through his weapon of deceit. If we are being pressed by him, we need to turn the tables and start to press him!

If we abide in Jesus by abiding in His Word, God makes us a promise that we will have the desires of our heart (Psalm 37:4). What a wonderful thing it is to know that giving heed to Jesus, obeying His every word, guarantees our abundant life in all circumstances.

Giving heed to Jesus guarantees our abundant life.

God's Kind of Success

This is the type of success that the world seeks but can never find, because it can only be found in Jesus.

The world's success, based on fame and fortune, is as fleeting as the wind. There is abundant evidence that

The world's success, based on fame and fortune, is as fleeting as the wind.

the lives of those who achieve this sort of success often end in tragic circumstances. Many celebrities seek direction through all the wrong avenues and become involved in things that are an abomination to God.

God commands us to have nothing to do with magic, astrology, fortune-telling, necromancy, tarot card reading, divining, clairvoyance and every other occult practice typical of the New Age movement. Without exception, there is nothing godly about any of these dealings with the demonic world through the operation of familiar spirits. The only Spirit we need to contact is the Holy Spirit of God, and He comes at no cost to bring His constant love, presence and assurance.

> *Blessed is the man who walks not in the counsel of the ungodly, nor stands in the path of sinners, nor sits in the seat of the scornful; but his delight is in the law of the Lord, and in his law he meditates day and night. He shall be like a tree planted by the rivers of water ... and whatever he does shall prosper. (Psalm 1:1–3)*

GOALS FULFIL PURPOSE

It is so important for people to have a purpose in life. So many young people are suicidal because they don't have a purpose. Prisons are full of people whose lives have never had any purpose or goal.

Jesus fulfilled His purpose so that we could have a purpose—a reason to get up every day and breathe the air afresh because His love is new every morning. He has given us a purpose to live. He has given us a destiny.

Jesus fulfilled His purpose so that we could have a purpose.

But we need to take hold of this destiny. Doing this involves developing particular goals within the framework of our overall destiny to live an abundant life. A goal is *a purpose out in front of you*. Habakkuk 2:2 says: '*Write the vision, and make it plain on tablets, that he may run who reads it*'. I have often found it helpful to write down my goals.

I remember when I first realised the importance of goals. My life was a mess. I had a great husband and four lovely children, but I did not know how to organise it all. I had to get my family responsibilities in order—that became one of my goals.

I also needed a goal for healing. Insomnia, depression and an incurable heart condition all gave way before the power of God as I confessed His Word in the context of a clear purpose to live in health.

Again, I started to see myself preaching. Humanly speaking it was impossible. I hated public speaking. It would hurt me to share Jesus because my life was such a mess. But I adopted a goal there, confessed God's Word that He had not given me a spirit of fear, and watched as God brought it about in my life.

CHOOSE A CONTENTED LIFE

All knowledge and wisdom have their ultimate source in God. The Bible shows us error to avoid, sin to forsake, examples to copy and promises to proclaim. If we allow God's Word to bring us necessary correction, restraint and instruction in His ways, we will live a contented and satisfied life.

We all need someone to point out areas where we may be missing it. Once when I was playing tennis, my backhand was off, and I needed my coach to show me what I was doing wrong. I had developed a wrong action that was not apparent to me—until it came unstuck under pressure in a big match. I took a whole week off and spent time going back to the basics and learning all over again how to hit the ball powerfully, efficiently and effectively. Once again it became my most formidable weapon. My place of defeat became my place of victory.

This can happen to us in our everyday lives. Sometimes we feel that we are doing all right in the game of life—until the pressure is on and we come unstuck.

If we ask God, He will be our coach, take us aside and ever so gently show us where we have been missing it. Through His Holy Spirit, He can show us as His children how to use His Word powerfully, efficiently and effectively to overcome our current distress and any future battle we face.

I have always preferred winning over losing, prosperity over poverty, health over sickness. If God's Word shows me what to do to ensure that type of success in my life, I would be very foolish not to obey it!

CHAPTER 7
WINNING WORDS TO HEALTH

My words ... are life to those who find them, and health to all their flesh.
(Proverbs 4:24)

Sometimes I still try to play tennis like I'm an eighteen year old, and when I do I can get very sore. This body of mine has had a lot of use over the years! I remember a few years ago I started to get particularly sore in the hips. But I'd learned enough about the power of God's Word to say, 'Hip trouble: you're on Jesus' hips, not mine. You can't stay in this body. I'll play tennis until the day I go home and be with the Lord.'

I've got no hip trouble today.

Jesus, the Bible says, *'took our infirmities and bore our sicknesses'* (Matthew 8:17). I teach a lot about health and healing because the principles of speaking in faith are so clear in this area. What you teach about healing covers every area: prosperity, family, marriage, depression, fear and much, much more.

I've already mentioned the time in my life when I was so sick I nearly gave up living. I was depressed, exhausted from insomnia and had a torn heart valve. The doctors gave me no hope of recovery from my heart condition, and I was filled with fear at the prospect that I would have to live with it for the rest of my life.

Then in 1980 I began to hear the good news that, as a child of God, healing belonged to me. The price Jesus paid 2,000 years ago included not only forgiveness for my sins but also deliverance from every other effect of evil in my life:

> *Surely He has borne our griefs and carried our sorrows ... He was wounded for our transgressions, He was bruised for our iniquities; the chastisement for our peace was upon Him, and by His stripes we are healed. (Isaiah 53:4–5)*

God had already done all He would ever do about our healing. I needed to grow in faith through the Word of God so I could reach out and receive it.

God has already done all He will ever do about our healing.

I did not know how this could happen, but I began to get hold of the truth that I needed to study and apply God's Word to my life. I took Philippians 4:13 and started to say it: 'I can do all things through Christ who strengthens me'. Then I started to say 2 Timothy 1:7, personalising it: 'I haven't got a spirit of fear but of power and love and a sound mind'. I started to meditate on Isaiah 53:4–5, putting 'I' and 'my' in it: 'Surely He has borne *my* griefs and carried *my* sorrows. ... He was wounded for *my* transgressions, He was bruised for *my* iniquities; the chastisement for *my* peace was upon Him, and by His stripes *I* am healed'.

Gradually I started to know on the inside of me that Jesus didn't just die for my sins, but that every whiplash on His back was for every part of my life—for healing, deliverance, safety, soundness, wholeness. I was feeding myself God's Word as medicine. As I heard it, God was creating in me the faith I needed to be able to believe things that didn't make sense to my mind and reason. I was discovering that there is life in His Word to transform situations that no doctor, counsellor or psychologist can change.

GETTING A PICTURE OF HEALING

I knew I had to get a clear picture of a healthy heart on which to focus my thoughts and speech. I had thought for so long about my torn heart valve that this was the only image I had. And the only words I had were words of fear that told me I would probably be on medication for the rest of my life. To be able to visualise healing I needed to see a healthy heart and to train every thought, word and deed in the direction of healing. Until I could see my healing with the eye of faith, and train myself to believe in it with every fibre of my being, there was no way I could receive it.

I got a picture of a healthy heart from an encyclopaedia and left it open on the hall table. I studied it every day until I could close my eyes and see that healthy heart. Every time I passed that open book I would say, 'This is a picture of my heart. I have healthy valves, arteries and blood vessels; my heart is strong and healthy and operating the way it was created by God to operate. I thank you, Lord Jesus, that my heart is healed today'. When doubt came to tell me that I was not healed—for I certainly did not feel or look healed—I would go to my picture and repeat the words that lined up with scriptural truth.

The only basis I had to believe I was healed was the Word of God. At one point a man of God laid hands on me according to Mark 16:18, which says that believers can lay hands on the sick and see them recover. From that moment onwards, I refused to believe anything other than that I was healed. After all, didn't God say that His words would be health to all my flesh (Proverbs 4:24)? An alternative translation for the Hebrew word 'health' here is 'medicine'—so I was taking the Word as medicine!

The only basis I had to believe I was healed was the Word of God.

My head tried on many occasions to talk me into being realistic, for it was obvious I was not actually healed. Faith, however, is not of the head but of the heart. So I could not afford to listen to my unrenewed mind or physical flesh, which were still operating in the realm of the five senses. God had said in His Word that He had healed me, and it was up to me to keep that vision of health and strength in both my natural and spiritual sights all the time.

God created the natural world from the supernatural

world through faith, which He released by His words. I started to see that I, too, was creating my desired natural world of good health from the supernatural world as I released my faith through my mouth.

The wonderful day of total healing came about six months after I first began to put the Word into my life on a consistent daily basis. I was desperate, and I'm glad I was—I may not have 'fought the good fight of faith' if I had just accepted my dreadful situation as the way things were always going to be.

Two years later I went to the doctors and they did tests of all kinds. They said, 'You're in perfect health'.

(Please don't think I'm saying you should throw away your medical treatments. You need to keep taking the doctor's medication until Jesus' medication overtakes it!)

HEALING BELONGS TO US

Healing belongs to us! We need to see that Jesus paid a price for our healing on the Cross. As Christians we understand that we are saved and destined for heaven. But there has been little teaching about the healing God provided for us through the sacrifice of His Son.

God has declared that we live in a land of perfect health, free from the giants of sickness and disease. It's up to us to appropriate that promise through our words. We will never walk in health until we speak health.

We will never walk in health until we speak health.

We saw in chapter 4 that Joshua and Caleb understood the principle of speaking in faith on the basis of God's promises. Their 'good report' took God at His word and refused to believe anything except what He said, whatever the circumstances. I like the admonition God gave to Joshua when he was about to take over from Moses and finally lead the Israelites into the Promised Land. Having Moses open the Red Sea was a bit of a hard act to follow, so first God told Joshua to *'be strong and of good courage'*. Then He went on:

> *'Only be strong and very courageous, that you may observe to do according to all the law which Moses My servant commanded you ... This Book of the Law shall not depart from your* mouth, *but you shall meditate in it day and night, that you may observe to do according to all that is written in it. For then you will make your way prosperous, and then you will have good success.' (Joshua 1:7–8)*

If Joshua needed to keep God's Word in his mouth and heart to make his way successful, how much more do we need to do the same to be successful against our enemies—whether they be depression, heart trouble or any other illness?

WALKING IN HEALTH

Often we get the question of healing back to front. We think we are the sick trying to get well, but we are not. We are the healed maintaining health.

God has won health for us through the Cross. He has already given it to us by grace. And as we receive it by faith we walk in the fullness of it.

We are not the sick trying to get well. We are the healed maintaining health.

It is God's will for health to flow in your life.

Many of us have been taught that sickness is God's way of teaching us things. But good parents don't hit their children over the head with a cricket bat or break their arm to teach them something, and God is no different. He is not out to get you. He is not trying to hit you over the head with cancer or arthritis or back pain to teach you something. He did not create what is wrong in your life (though He may use it). God is not out to destroy you or tear you apart.

God loves you, and He desires for you complete health and wholeness. God wants to heal you.

I'm not saying you should deny that sickness is there. Sickness is real. Pain is real. But when people come to you and ask how you are, say, 'Well, I believe I'm healed because the Word of God says I'm healed. Jesus took my infirmities and sicknesses. Healing belongs to me.'

That's speaking of things that are not, as if they are.

Every time you think of the negative (your fears, a doctor's poor diagnosis, the doubts of others), swing it around to the positive (God's Word). The more you speak about the problem, the more you will be held in bondage to it. And if you are tempted to say, 'It's too hard', say instead, 'I can do all things through Christ who strengthens me' and, 'I'm more than a conqueror through Him who loves me'. The more we say it's too hard, the harder it will get.

Speak words of health and life, not words of sickness and defeat. If you speak contrary to God's Word by speaking of things as they are, instead of as they are not, then you will see no change. God sees us well, because healing is part of our full atonement. But if we call ourselves sick, tired and depressed that is what we will be. We can't live above the words of our mouth.

BELIEVING BEFORE SEEING

To see how powerful for healing God's words can be, we need only look at the scriptural example of the Roman centurion who came to Jesus and asked for his servant to be healed.

> *Now when Jesus had entered Capernaum, a centurion came to Him, pleading with Him, saying, 'Lord, my servant is lying at home paralyzed, dreadfully tormented.'*
>
> *And Jesus said to him, 'I will come and heal him.'*
>
> *The centurion answered and said, 'Lord, I am not worthy that You should come under my roof. But only speak a word, and my servant will be healed. For I also am a man under authority, having soldiers under me. And I say to this one, "Go," and he goes;*

and to another, "Come," and he comes; and to my servant, "Do this," and he does it.'

When Jesus heard it, He marvelled, and said to those who followed, 'Assuredly, I say to you, I have not found such great faith, not even in Israel!' . . .

Then Jesus said to the centurion, 'Go your way; and as you have believed, so let it be done for you.' And his servant was healed that same hour. (Matthew 8:8–10, 13)

The centurion was under authority, had authority and knew about authority. This man took Jesus at His word, recognising Him to be a man of authority and believing He would do what He said He would do. He knew the words Jesus spoke were words of authority that he could stand and act on without disappointment. He had no need to touch, see or feel the healing of his servant before he believed; he believed before he could see any sign of change or healing.

We too need to take God's Word as our first and final authority. It doesn't matter what the circumstances say; it's always what God says that ultimately will matter in our lives. This is faith at its highest, for eventually the confession of our faith—God's Word continually coming out of our mouth—will bring about the thing hoped for.

It is always what God says that ultimately matters in our lives.

PRINCIPLES FOR HEALING

There are certain principles to follow when we desire healing for our bodies. We need to *hear*, *speak*, *act* and *receive*. Nowhere is this better seen than in the story of the woman with the flow of blood (Mark 5:25–34).

> *Now a certain woman had a flow of blood for twelve years, and had suffered many things from many physicians. She had spent all that she had and was no better.*

This woman was suffering in every aspect of her life because of her physical condition. I know what this is like because when I was sick it affected every part of my life too. Emotionally she suffered the torment of being ostracised by society, for by religious law she was considered unfit to be on the streets. Financially she was broke because she had spent everything seeking a cure from doctors. Years had been wasted looking for help from those who could not help, despite her hopes. And she lived constantly with the pain and distress of the continual bleeding.

She was being robbed of her life and there was no good news ahead for her—until she heard about Jesus.

Jesus was teaching that He was anointed by God to heal all those who were oppressed by the devil. She realised that Jesus was the key to her healing. This was good news indeed! The words He spoke and the words she heard created enough faith in her to believe that if she could just get to Him, she would be made well.

> *When she* heard *about Jesus, she came behind Him in the crowd and* touched *His garment; for she* said *'If only I may touch His clothes, I shall be made well.'*

She acted by reaching out to Jesus and she received. Step 1: She heard. Step 2: She spoke in faith. Step 3: She acted. Step 4: She received her healing. We see the wonderful result of her taking the all-important leap of faith and acting on what she said in the very next verse:

> *Immediately the fountain of her blood was dried up, and she felt in her body that she was healed of the affliction.*

THE TOUCH OF FAITH

So that future generations could see what actually took place in her healing, and by what method it was done, Jesus turned around in front of the whole crowd and asked who it was that had touched Him. Her touch was different from the touch of everyone else who had reached out to Him that day.

What made her touch different was that it was a touch of faith. She fully believed that what she had spoken would come to pass, otherwise her act of touching the hem of His garment would have been a meaningless display of hope. But she put her faith to the ultimate test, for if she had been discovered on the streets with a flow of blood she faced death by stoning.

God is compelled to comply with the demands that we make on Him through our faith. I don't mean we should arrogantly think we can force God to act on our behalf, for He is God and He is sovereign. But we do honour and respect Him when we believe and act on His Word regardless of our situation, and our faith pleases Him.

And Jesus, immediately knowing in Himself that power had gone out of Him, turned around in the crowd and said, 'Who touched my clothes?'

There is something about the touch of faith that gets God's attention every time. God responds to those who make withdrawals of His power through their faith. This woman acted on what Jesus said He was anointed to do. In one touch of faith, she deposited her sickness into Him and took from Him the spiritual power needed to destroy the 'yoke' of sickness that weighed down her life.

There is something about the touch of faith that gets God's attention every time.

Jesus was quite clear about the reason for her success:

And He said to her, 'Daughter, your faith has made you well. Go in peace, and be healed of your affliction.'

It was *her* faith that made her well, not His. Our faith pleases God because, on the basis of our faith, He can move to bring about everything we firmly believe. If we *hear* the words of Jesus, *believe* the words of Jesus, *speak out* our faith in the words of Jesus and *act* on the words of Jesus, we will receive from God the things we believe for.

A MODERN MIRACLE

When I was in South Africa in 1994, I prayed for a young girl named Nikki who had a similar condition to this woman.

Her development had stopped at the age of four and she had begun to spot bleed. This condition had persisted, and when she was 15, tests revealed that Nikki had no right ovary, her left ovary was undeveloped and her uterus was only as big as a thumbnail. Her pituitary gland was not producing the hormones needed for normal bodily development. She was told she would never have a child and would remain on hormone tablets for the rest of her life.

Nikki's mother brought her to a meeting where she heard I would be ministering. Looking back, she says she just *knew* this was where Nikki would be healed! At the end of the meeting I made the following altar call: 'Would all those people to whom the doctors have said, "There is nothing more we can do for you and you will have to be on medication for the rest of your life", come to the front now, because Jesus wants to heal you!'

Her mother knew that this was the night for Nikki,

so she brought the young girl forward. I laid hands on her. I did not know it at the time, but apparently the bleeding ceased from that point onwards—twelve long and painful years after it first began.

Afterwards, tests revealed that Nikki had been miraculously healed. Where once she had only one poor ovary, now there are two fully developed and functional ovaries, and a normal sized uterus. She is perfectly capable of becoming a mother and reproducing life from her once dead and diseased womb.

Nikki and her mother came that night with the same faith that the woman in the Bible had. The results were the same. They both received what they desired—through a touch of faith.

Jesus can still be touched today, simply by acting in faith on His Word.

CHAPTER 8

WINNING WORDS TO RIGHTEOUSNESS

For He made Him who knew no sin to be sin for us, that we might become the righteousness of God in Him.
(2 Corinthians 5:21)

Those of us who are children of God know we don't deserve to be called righteous, but the wonderful fact is that God does call us righteous because He sees us through the Cross of Jesus. The full price for our salvation has been paid. We are no longer working out our own righteousness by trying to earn what God has already freely given to us.

The Father wants all of His children to learn who they really are in Jesus, what they can have in Him and what they can be in Him. If we have this basic knowledge of our righteousness, we will begin to transform our image of ourselves into the image that God has of us.

The world has given us a mostly negative image of ourselves. Few of us escape childhood without damage to our self-esteem, perceptions and personalities. The image we form is far below the image that God has of us. To Him we are valuable, precious and worthy of such great love that He gave His Son for us. Jesus became sin so that we could become righteous.

God sees us as happy, healthy and prosperous in all we do. He says we can do all things (in line with His will) because we have a covenant with Him and He is our all-powerful, loving heavenly Father.

God sees us as happy, healthy and prosperous in all we do.

Sadly, many of us never realise that this is God's image of us and never come to share that image of ourselves. I can see myself this way today, but there was a time when I felt like an absolute worm. Every time I walked into a church I wanted to crawl under the carpet. And I had no idea I should never have felt this way at all.

MY 'RAGS OF RIGHTEOUSNESS'

I was brought up in a religious environment without ever knowing that some of the practices, doctrines and beliefs I followed were not based on the Scriptures. Constant repentance in the confessional kept me aware that I was a sinner and totally unworthy of God's attention. I felt I had to work hard all the time to please Him, yet, although my transgressions seemed few, I cannot remember ever feeling that I achieved this.

Right from childhood through adolescence and into adulthood, I felt insignificant, full of guilt and the consciousness of sin. I never really felt right until I did what I thought I needed to do to feel right. This was legalism in operation. I knew nothing about the grace of God or His abundant mercy for my mistakes. I always felt condemned, even when I was doing what was right.

I was dressed in my own 'rags of righteousness' instead of Jesus' robes of righteousness. Like blind Bartimaeus, who had the sense to cast aside his dirty, beggarly garb to rise from the dust when Jesus touched his life, I too should have been able to cast aside my old beggarly garments of sin and unworthiness under Jesus' touch. Unfortunately, I did not even know this was possible.

My problem was that I had no knowledge of the Scriptures. The only time I recall hearing the Bible was during the Gospel reading of the day. I loved this part of the service when the priest read the Bible aloud. I never had a Bible of my own, for the simple reason we never used one in any of our various church-centred activities. Consequently, I had very limited knowledge of God, and even less of my real enemy, the devil. God was presented as far too stern a taskmaster for me to ever think I could approach Him, and the only mention of the devil was in relation to not wanting to end up with him in the fires of hell!

In all the thirty years before I was saved I never heard that I needed to be 'born again'. I thought my baptism as an infant was enough to save me. And if my good deeds outweighed my sins, the balance would be enough to let me into heaven. Even if I did not make it through heaven's doors the first time around, there would be enough rosaries and novenas said on earth by others to influence God to let me suffer just a little for my sins and then go on to glory.

It came as quite a surprise to learn that if I did not know I was going to heaven by being born again, there was a fair chance I would not be going! I had never learned from God's Word that, while my infant water baptism was symbolic of my dedication to Christ, it had not brought me into God's salvation. I was ignorant of the basic facts of how to be saved:

Whoever calls on the name of the Lord shall be saved. (Romans 10:13)

That which is born of the flesh is flesh, and that which is born of the Spirit is spirit . . . You must be born again. (John 3:6–7)

For by grace you have been saved through faith, and that not of yourselves; it is the gift of God, not of works, lest anyone should boast. (Ephesians 2:8–9)

We can't be saved unless we *hear* that we need to be saved. When we hear the uncompromised Word, it creates faith in us to enable us to break free from our reasoning, doubts and unbelief so that we can accept Jesus as our Lord and Saviour. Unless we hear of our need to be born again, we may blindly continue in our traditions, ceremonies and religious church-going, ignorant of the peace, joy and righteousness that comes with true salvation.

We can't be saved unless we* hear *that we need to be saved.

GROWING AS A NEW CREATION

If we need to hear the Word of God to be saved, we also need to hear it to grow as a new creation. Although receiving Jesus as Lord was the most wonderful experience of my life, my ignorance of God's Word and His true character greatly hindered my growth in the early years of my Christian life.

I was a Christian, but a sick and fearful one. Even though I loved God and knew that I was heaven-bound, I was living a defeated life. It was hard to reconcile the words of Jesus with my experience when I prayed the Lord's Prayer, for it was obvious I was missing out on the reality of that part of the prayer that says, '*Your will be done here on earth as it is in heaven*'. 'Here on earth' had become equivalent to 'hell on earth' for me, and if it was going to get any worse I really did not want to go on living. Heaven had to be better than this!

I had no idea how to overcome the adversity I encountered in my life as a Christian. Just as I had been ignorant of what God's Word said about becoming His child, so I was ignorant of what it said about how God saw me—the basic reality that I was a spirit who lived in a body and had a soul. Like God Himself, I was three-in-one, and I could only be whole when all three parts of my being were in harmony. It was a turning point for me the day I discovered 1 Thessalonians 5:23:

> *Now may the God of peace Himself sanctify you completely; and may your whole spirit, soul, and*

body be preserved blameless at the coming of our Lord Jesus Christ.

I began to personalise this Scripture: 'I'm a spirit, I live in a body and I have a soul'. I kept saying it aloud to establish the reality of this new truth in my mind so that I could grasp its full significance. I had wrongly assumed I was just a body and a soul, not knowing that the soul and the spirit are not the same thing at all. In Hebrews it tells us that the Word of God can actually *divide* between our spirit and soul:

You are a spirit, you live in a body and you have a soul.

For the word of God is living and powerful, and sharper than any two-edged sword, piercing even to the division of soul and spirit, and of joints and marrow, and is a discerner of the thoughts and intents of the heart. (Hebrews 4:12)

I began to realise that I could either live out of my soul—that is, on the basis of my own reasonings and emotions—or out of my newly created spirit. And it was the Word that would show me the difference.

One night in my prayer time, I 'saw' myself and another 'me' standing beside me. Instantly I knew that this person standing right next to me, looking just as I did in form and substance, was the 'real me'—my 'spirit man'. This 'spirit man' was a happy, healthy and vibrant 'me', for it was in my spirit that the wonderful miracle of salvation had taken place. But the other 'me' was my 'flesh man', and this 'flesh man' was still characterised by sin, sickness and turmoil of mind. It stood in front of my new 'spirit man', dominating it.

Then the picture changed. As I started to feed my 'spirit man' with God's Word day and night, the sin, sickness and mental turmoil lost their position of dominance and the 'spirit man' started to rise up and become dominant. The more I heard of God's Word, the more power my 'spirit man' exercised over my 'flesh man', until the 'flesh man' was successfully controlled.

The Word of God enabled me to see myself as I truly was. As I began to live out of my new spirit, strengthened by the Word, my life began to change. I was no longer dominated by the thoughts and emotions of defeat, negativity and fear.

A Man with a New Spirit

One of the clearest examples I have seen of the liberation that comes when we begin to see ourselves as God sees us was a man who had been an alcoholic for over twenty years. He came to one of my meetings desperately seeking help.

His addiction had cost him everything he held dear: his marriage, home, children and money. He had spent a great deal of time in psychiatric counselling attempting to discern the reason for his problem. These sessions gave him many plausible and logical reasons for his drinking, but they could not offer him any way to overcome it. Alcoholics Anonymous and other groups similarly failed. Talking about his drinking and the terrible guilt he felt only led him further into captivity to it. Frequently he went straight from meetings to do what he felt so bad about doing but could not stop.

When he heard my explanation about being a spirit being, living in a body and having a soul, he instantly recognised the source of his struggle. He realised that he would be able to overcome his horrible addiction through the strength of his spirit empowered by the Holy Spirit. He gave his heart to Jesus in a true show of repentant tears and on the spot became a brand new creature in Christ. Now he instinctively knew he had the power of God to help him overcome this dreadful and debilitating sin.

It did not happen overnight. He had to change the way he saw himself and the way he had always acted before he could say goodbye to the craving for alcohol that had driven him to despair over two long decades. But he had a new spirit, the Holy Spirit, living inside him, and with that power available to him it was only a short time before he began to live the righteous way he was always meant to live.

His old friends were amazed—especially when they saw their former drinking mate go off to Bible School and faithfully complete three years of study!

CHANGE FROM THE INSIDE

The dominance of our new 'spirit man' by our old 'flesh man' is the primary obstacle to growing in righteousness. Christians often get caught somewhere between the way of the world and the way of God. Even though we are spiritually alive to God, our minds and bodies can still be thinking and acting in the world's way. You don't wash away years of unbelief, tradition and bad habits overnight. It takes time—and lots of attention to God's Word.

Christians often get caught somewhere between the way of the world and the way of God.

We need to hear enough of God's Word to effect a complete turn around in our lives. Our heart needs to become fully established in our new identity so that more and more we live under the prompting of our 'spirit man'.

We need to hear enough of God's Word to effect a complete turn around in our lives.

For centuries religion has preached the wrong message. It has tried to clean us up on the outside without cleaning us up on the inside. 'Clean up your act ... stop drinking ... don't smoke ... stop sleeping around ... don't take drugs ... stop stealing—and then maybe God will accept, love and save you.' This is what Christians have preached. We have been ignorant of God's grace that tells us Jesus died for us *while we were still in our sin*. He did not wait for us to get right with Him before He drew us to Himself. He wants us now, just as we are!

If we are in sin we can start to change straight away. He will give us the strength to overcome any area which has a hold on us. As we grow in the knowledge of our righteousness in Christ—of who we are and what we can do in Him—we gain real strength to resist sin in all its deadly forms. The outer man changes as the inner man is transformed. Both the world and religion try to change people from the outside in, but until you change a person's heart you can't change the outside. At best it's a religious exercise in looking and acting okay, but the core of the problem remains untouched.

Until you change a person's heart you cannot change the outside.

Hurting people hurt people because they don't know any other way. They have to be shown their worth and what they can become. In essence, they need to know someone believes in them and cares deeply for them. And that's what God does!

Newness in Every Part of Us

The basis for this growth in righteousness is the righteousness of Jesus. When we come to Jesus *as the sinners we are*, not on the basis of our supposed good deeds, He immediately exchanges our sin for His righteousness and washes us whiter than snow (Isaiah 1:18). Our sins are forgiven and forgotten.

Without knowing our righteousness in Christ I do not believe any Christian can have confidence and faith in God. God has shown me the importance of taking not just His free gift of salvation, but also the sense of true righteousness, for without it there will be no victory. Salvation doesn't automatically bring us into that place of victory. We need to stand in our righteousness to claim our full inheritance in God.

It is a wonderful thing. The renewal that flows from this gift touches every area of our being.

Our spirit. As I have noted many times, when someone becomes God's child, the Spirit of God makes their spirit alive. It is reborn, and the Holy Spirit comes to live within them:

But he who is joined to the Lord is one spirit with Him. (1 Corinthians 6:17)

. . . if the Spirit of Him who raised Jesus from the dead dwells in you, He who raised Christ from the dead will also give life to your mortal bodies through His Spirit who dwells in you. (Romans 8:10–11)

Our soul (mind). There is nothing naturally good in the mind. It's a part of us that is subject to sin and death. If left alone, the mind will take the path of least resistance and indulge its every desire. This is what the Bible calls living 'according to the flesh', and there is a price to pay for it.

But if we live under the control of the Holy Spirit operating through our own born again spirit, we will be free from the curse of sin and death. Then the mind can be renewed or 'reprogrammed' according to God's Word.

An example of how this works is forgiveness. Our natural minds often want to harbour feelings of hate and unforgiveness towards others, but both the Word of God and our renewed spirits tell us that we are to forgive those who hurt us:

> *And whenever you stand praying, if you have anything against anyone, forgive him, that your Father in heaven may also forgive you your trespasses. (Mark 11:25)*

Many people tell me they can't forgive. The truth is they can forgive, but won't. God says they can!

You may not feel like forgiving, but you need to make up your mind that you will. By feeding your spirit on God's words about forgiving others, you will be strengthened to reject your mind's natural inclination to harbour resentment, hatred and revenge.

Our body. Just like the mind, the body is not naturally attracted to disciplines for its own well-being. Doctors tell us that many people are sick because of poor eating and exercise habits. The body loves to be pampered. High on its list of preferred activities are binge chocolate sessions propped up on the sofa watching TV, remote control in hand.

Our bodies, like our minds, are naturally tuned to the sin and death in the world. Without God we have a challenge on our hands to change our behaviour. But with God we can train ourselves by His Word to live a disciplined and controlled life.

DEALING WITH OUR TOUGHEST DIFFICULTIES

Having a disciplined mind in a disciplined body, with both mind and body submitted to a re-created spirit, is paramount for success in every area. From this comes a spiritual reality that powerfully deals with our toughest difficulties. For example:

Temptations that beguile us. Paul tells us to '*Awake to righteousness, and do not sin*' (1 Corinthians 15:34). We must wilfully resolve to do what is right because it's right, and most of us want to. But how?

Our real problem lies in resisting temptations to do what is wrong instead of what is right. These temptations are centred in our 'flesh' (that is, in our unredeemed mind and body). Our spirit cannot sin.

Temptation is simply a strong pull towards our own particular desires. A few temptations, such as selfishness, self-centredness and greed, arise on a constant basis and need to be constantly resisted. We are not alone in this dilemma, for the Apostle Paul faced the same problem:

> *For the good that I will to do, I do not do; but the evil I will not to do, that I practise ... O wretched man that I am! Who will deliver me from this body of death? (Romans 7:19, 25)*

As we establish our heart's new spiritual identity through the Word of God, trying to do what is right comes not so much from an act of willpower but from a strengthening of our walk and talk with God. God's Word shows us that overcoming any evil, whether it be sickness, grief, depression, lack, worry or sin, is far easier if we build ourselves into His strength than into our own.

We can choke all our old cares, worries and anxieties through the Word.

Worries that trouble us. We can choke all our old cares, worries and anxieties through the Word. I will say more about this in the next chapter, but notice this wonderful promise from God:

Be anxious for nothing, but in everything by prayer and supplication, with thanksgiving, let your requests be made known to God; and the peace of God, which surpasses all understanding, will guard your hearts and minds through Christ Jesus. (Philippians 4:6–7)

Personally, it was through God's Word that I learned to speak back to all the problems that were always speaking to me. Every time thoughts of defeat rose up in me—'You're never going to make it ... You're getting weaker ... You'll never play tennis again ... You're going to die of a heart attack'—I would say, 'No! I can do all things through Christ who

It was through God's Word that I learned to speak back to the problems that were always speaking to me.

strengthens me', again and again, until those fearful thoughts were dead and buried.

I did this all the time, whenever evil thoughts came, and I entertained fewer and fewer words of defeat.

Developing the fruit of the Spirit. When you first accept Jesus as Lord, the fruit of the Spirit come into your life. You might say, for example, that you don't have any love, but when you received Jesus, the love of God was shed abroad in your heart (Romans 5:5). You might not be *walking* in that love, but it is there. And you can develop it.

It takes time for the fruit to grow, of course. When you plant seed in the ground to grow vegetables, it takes time to see the fullness of the fruit. But the seeds are there, even when the fruit is not obvious.

How do you cultivate the fruit of the Spirit? You start by speaking. When you begin to say what God says about you—what He says about the love He has placed in your heart, for example—an image will form of that fruit in your life. You will be able to picture it. Then you will be able to believe it. And then it will grow.

BREAKING FREE FROM CONDEMNATION

One problem that was particularly important for me to escape was self-condemnation. This was one of my big struggles, as I described at the start of this chapter.

The Apostle Paul was quick to learn that the only way he could escape the condemnation of his past was to look forward every day to his new life in Christ:

Brethren, I do not count myself to have apprehended; but one thing I do, forgetting those things which are behind and reaching forward to those things which are ahead, I press toward the goal for the prize of the upward call of God in Christ Jesus. (Philippians 3:13–14)

When God impressed on me that in Christ '*old things have passed away and all things have become new*' (2 Corinthians 5:17), I realised I had the key to dealing with condemnation. Every time self-condemning thoughts came to me, I would say, 'Nope! Yesterday's gone. Old things have passed away, all things have become new. I'm a new creature in Christ Jesus'. I repeated it over and over again until the Word of God choked the weed and drove it right out of my life.

When you think and speak that way to the things that hold you captive, the wonderful day comes when you look for them and say, 'Where are they? Were they really ever part of my life?'

BREAKING FREE FROM THE PAST

The same is true of the things people have done to us. Tragically, many people want to wallow in the grief and injustices of the past. They love going back over the old. They embrace it; it's part of their life.

The past may have been sad or tragic, but it is worse to stay imprisoned by it. We can try to live our past in our present, but it will steal our wonderful future from us.

The past is finished. Let God avenge you and bring to justice those who have in any way done evil to you. If you will let it go you will be free of it, and all of the unforgiveness, bitterness, anger, hurt, rejection, jealousy and grief will not poison your life.

We can try to live our past in our present, but it will steal our wonderful future from us.

Thankfully most of us desire to leave behind the old and go on with the new. There is little behind us worth hanging on to. Good memories are fine, but sad and tragic memories are better forgotten. The only way to truly forget the past is to fully immerse ourselves in God's Word and see the wonderful future He has ahead for every one of us. It's not how we begin that counts but how we finish.

The only way to truly forget the past is to fully immerse ourselves in God's Word.

The ability to truly put off the old life is a wonderful thing. Most of us have suffered to some degree through the world's tangled web of sickness, despair and pain. To look forward with expectancy and total faith in God, knowing our life can be worth living and living well, brings joy, peace and contentment that the world knows nothing about.

For I know the thoughts that I think towards you, says the Lord, thoughts of peace and not of evil, to give you a future and a hope. (Jeremiah 29:11)

Chapter 9

Winning Words to Peace and Security

God has not given us a spirit of fear, but of power and of love and of a sound mind.
(2 Timothy 1:7)

Genuine peace comes from God alone. Only God, who loves and accepts each of us as precious individuals, is able to give us true significance and security. Without Him we will only experience the fleeting significance and false security that the world has to offer. There is no lasting peace in any of it.

Even if we think we know God, if we don't know His Word, our lives will be constantly pitted with fear, frustration, anxiety, stress, heartache and worry—all the symptoms of a world in turmoil. But if we renew our minds by feeding God's Word into our spirit, we will be able to tear down every thought, fear, worry or anxiety that is against God's peace and security and make them captive to Christ:

For the weapons of our warfare are not carnal but mighty in God for pulling down strongholds, casting down arguments and every high thing that exalts itself against the knowledge of God, bringing every thought into captivity to the obedience of Christ. (2 Corinthians 10:4–5)

Fear, the Enemy of Peace

We move through life with one of two forces dominating our experience—faith or fear. Faith takes us to victory. Fear takes us to defeat. And we instinctively know (for they are spiritual forces) which one is operating in us at any given time.

We move through life with one of two forces dominating our experience—faith or fear.

I have already related in chapter 2 how many of my mother's fears were passed on to me. What she said was a reflection of her own fear and torment living in a household where alcohol was abused. My birth was difficult—she almost died during labour and there was no guarantee I would survive beyond the first day. From that time on, most of the words she spoke to me were tinged with her fear that something bad was going to happen to me.

This fear about me was just one of the fears that coloured my mother's whole existence. She would seldom leave the house, and when she did it was fleeting. Fear that something had been left burning on the stove, or that the iron had been left on, would ruin our family outings on a regular basis because she always insisted on returning home. I don't recall a time when we found the stove or iron on.

My mother loved me very much and did not realise what she was doing to me. But what she said gradually became part of me. I became full of care and worry, just like she was. Fear of the dark; fear of strangers; fear of spiders; on and on it went. Fear of many things there was no need to fear!

My Terrified Heart

Becoming a Christian did not at first do anything to stop my fears. Rather the opposite. In my early Christian walk I came under a lot of wrong teaching that reinforced my old ways of thinking and acting. I felt nervous, unworthy, condemned and guilty all the time. Eventually my fear led, I believe, to the physical illnesses that nearly destroyed me.

I was a living picture of how the book of Deuteronomy describes those who do not truly know the Word of God and are not observing what it says:

Your life shall hang in doubt before you; you shall fear day and night, and have no assurance of life. In the morning you shall say, 'Oh, that it were evening!' And at evening you shall say, 'Oh, that it were morning!' because of the fear which terrifies your heart, and because of the sight which your eyes see. (Deuteronomy 28:66–67)

I did not know this Scripture was in the Bible at the time, but it was almost word perfect what I was constantly saying about myself.

Why was I like this? Because in my ignorance I had listened to the world's words, which create fear, and had never fed myself with God's Word, which creates faith. Sitting in a pew, going through a traditional way of worship, had done nothing to stop my fear and worry. I lacked knowledge, and such was my state of mind that, but for the Word of God changing my life, I would have finished up going home to be with the Lord or in a mental hospital.

THE TORMENT OF FEAR

Fear is torment. At the height of my suffering, my fear was so great I felt as if Satan was in the same room with me for two years. Night would come and I would wish it was morning. I would close my eyes and see faces laughing at me.

My fear was so great I felt as if Satan was in the same room with me for two years.

There are few things worse than the horrifying feeling that comes over you when fear takes charge. Your whole body is electrified as the adrenalin glands work overtime to accommodate a racing heart-rate. Emotions spin out of control. Your mind loses its ability for rational thought. Panic takes over. Sleep is impossible. You are on a merry-go-round with no off-switch.

Most fears are irrational, but to our way of thinking they are frighteningly real. When we speak we show the depth of our fearful hearts, for there is no way we will tell everyone we are happy, healthy and successful if we are in this dreadful condition.

When I was playing tennis, I often had such a bad case of nerves at Wimbledon that I almost could not walk onto centre court. The world sees pre-match nerves as quite natural in a sporting contest, believing them to be essential for the increased flow of adrenalin to the soon-to-be-working muscles. Supposedly, once play begins they are quickly dispersed as the mind and body focus on the task at hand. But at Wimbledon my pre-match nerves often lasted the whole game!

I recall one final at Wimbledon when I was so nervous I could not even throw the ball up straight to serve. I remember throwing up prayers to God instead, pleading with Him to help me get it right. How much better it would have been to go out there full of faith and confidence, realising that my self-worth was not tied to winning a tennis match, however important it appeared to be.

Fear is Satan's counterfeit of faith.

Many things fuel such fears. In my case, part of the cause was fear of failing, of performing badly and letting down so many people besides myself. But underneath it all, fear is a spiritual attack. For fear is Satan's counterfeit of faith.

FEAR IS THE PERVERSION OF FAITH

Despite what we are told, fear is not natural to human beings. No child is born fearful, as any mother can attest. We are all born with an abundance of faith and a belief that we can do anything and nothing can possibly hurt us. Children simply believe. And as children we find it easy to believe in God, for we are full of faith and confidence.

Fear is not natural. We are all born with an abundance of faith.

But then we grow and supposedly mature. We lose our child-like faith and it turns into its opposite—fear. God's truth that we can live without fear is replaced with the devil's lie that fear is natural.

Franklin D Roosevelt once said that the only thing we had to fear was fear itself. Understood in the light of God's Word, this is perhaps the most profound statement ever made about fear. The Bible says repeatedly to *'fear not'* (Genesis 26:24; Deuteronomy 31:8; Isaiah 41:10, 43:1). We see this command time and time again when God is about to do something miraculous or seemingly impossible in people's lives. He knows that fear in any form will stop the creative flow of His power. And so it is with us today. Where we have fear, we can't have faith.

Fear masquerades in many forms: anxiety, stress, worry, depression and care.

Natural reflexes or a quick surge to move us out of harm's way should not be confused with the spirit of fear, which is quite demonic. This type of fear takes on many forms: anxiety, stress, worry, depression and care—all the supposedly natural ills of our modern world. All are potential killers.

God doesn't create fear. He commands us to respect Him—that is, to stand in reverential awe before His majesty and might. But this is not fear. Fear is simply a perversion of faith. God has placed in us a natural ability to believe. When we fear, we place that God-given faith in the ability of something or somebody to rob, kill or destroy us.

God does not create fear. Fear is simply a perversion of faith.

BUILDING FEAR OR FAITH

Fear and faith both come through the words we hear. As we have seen throughout this book, our minds are very fertile and will produce a crop of anything they are consistently fed. Once a thought is entertained and mulled over, our imagination produces an image of that thought and before long it becomes reality.

Faith and fear both come through the words we hear.

This is powerfully true with fear. We watch the television news or read the newspapers, with their steady diet of tragedy and more tragedy, and it's not long before we are imagining the worst possible scenario in every situation. The fearful mother can see her toddler lying motionless on the road. The anxious father can picture his teenager lying in a car wreck. The child lost in the supermarket for just an instant is pictured abducted and even murdered.

Once we form these negative pictures we are living in fear.

But faith, too, grows from what we feed our minds. While my fear was well-developed through hearing my mother voice her anxieties, I did have faith in one area: my sport. And it came the way the Bible tells us faith comes, through hearing words.

When I was a young thirteen year old, Frank Sedgeman, a great Australian player, told me he believed I could become the first Australian woman to win Wimbledon. I spoke those words into my heart until I began to see myself actually standing on centre court at Wimbledon, holding the coveted trophy. I spoke about winning Wimbledon all the time, imagining how it would feel to win. When anyone asked me what I wanted to do with my tennis, I told them I wanted to be the first Australian woman to win Wimbledon.

My heart and my mouth lined up, and I just *knew* I would one day fulfil the image I could see so clearly. I never pictured defeat, so I automatically stopped speaking defeat. Every thought, word and deed was focussed on winning!

Of course, fears and doubts came. How did a scrawny teenager from an Australian country town think she was going to win Wimbledon? But the fears and doubts disappeared when I recalled Frank Sedgeman's words of encouragement and inspiration. If Mr Sedgeman believed I could do it, then I believed I could do it too! In the hard spots, his words came back to reassure me.

FEAR OUT, FAITH IN

I knew nothing about God's principles at that time, but I was applying them nonetheless and faith developed in me. Later I discovered that overcoming fear involved the same principles: hearing, picturing, believing.

Fear can only be cast out by perfect love.

Fear is so strong that nothing we can do in and of ourselves will rid us of it. It can only be cast out by perfect love:

> *There is no fear in love; but perfect love casts out fear, because fear involves torment. But he who fears has not been made perfect in love. (1 John 4:18)*

Perfect love comes from God, who pours His love into our hearts by His Spirit. He is the very opposite of fear:

> *For you did not receive the spirit of bondage again to fear, but you received the Spirit of adoption by whom we cry out, 'Abba, Father.' (Romans 8:15)*

Until you love and know God you will not be able to truly love yourself. But when you are secure in His love and in who you are in Him, you can be loosed from the negativity of the spirit of fear.

At the time of my sickness, I did not realise my problems were spiritual rather than physical. I had to be changed by the renewing of my mind. This renewing would only occur if I took my attention off my many problems and gave it to God's Word on a daily basis.

Do not be conformed to this world, but be transformed by the renewing of your mind, that you may prove what is that good and acceptable and perfect will of God. (Romans 12:2)

God's will for us is not tinged with fear, insecurity, despair and torment. His will is all good. He has provided a way of escape for everyone who seeks refuge in Him from the curse that is on the earth through the fallen nature of man. Our part is to 'prove' how good God's will is by renewing our minds through His Word. As we hear more and more of His Word, our faith grows and eventually brings God's will onto the earth in our lives.

I eventually learned to overcome my fear and mental torment by constantly feeding on God's Word, especially 2 Timothy 1:7:

God has not given us a spirit of fear, but of power and of love and of a sound mind.

This became my favourite Scripture and I hold it very dear to this day. It became the stabilising Word of God that anchored my troubled, tormented mind.

The transformation of anyone gripped by fear and anxiety begins when they ask Jesus, the Prince of Peace, into their life. Then the way is open for God's Word to have its powerful and healing impact. Like a beautiful butterfly, they will emerge from their former cocoon of fear into the love and faith that is in Christ Jesus.

THROW AWAY YOUR WORRY BEADS

Peace and security are easily undermined by one of the most common forms of fear: worry. Jesus said we are not to worry, focussing particularly on the everyday issues of what we will eat, drink and wear. He was telling us we can walk free from care:

Therefore I say to you, do not worry about your life, what you will eat or what you will drink; nor about your body, what you will put on. Is not life more than food and the body more than clothing? Look at the birds of the air, for they neither sow nor reap nor gather into barns; yet your heavenly Father feeds them. Are you not of more value than they?

Which of you by worrying can add one cubit to his stature? So why do you worry about clothing?

Consider the lilies of the field, how they grow: they neither toil nor spin; and yet I say to you that even Solomon in all his glory was not arrayed like one of these. Now if God so clothes the grass of the field, which today is, and tomorrow is thrown into the oven, will He not much more clothe you, O you of little faith?

Therefore do not worry, saying, 'What shall we eat?' or 'What shall we drink?' or 'What shall we wear?' For after all these things the Gentiles seek. For your heavenly Father knows that you need all these things. But seek first the kingdom of God and His righteousness, and all these things shall be added to you.

Therefore do not worry about tomorrow, for tomorrow will worry about its own things. Sufficient for the day is its own trouble. (Matthew 6:25–34)

Five times here Jesus says not to worry. Our heavenly Father knows everything we need, so we can confidently cast our cares on Him.

I have found that worry and care zero you in on yourself. When I started saying what God said about me and what Jesus had done for me on the Cross, it took my eyes off myself. I started looking out. Then I started giving out to others. And all the anxieties that had a hold on me began to fade.

Let the Word of God build you and mould you. Replace worry with God's Word. Here's a practical suggestion:

• Write out all your problems and cares on a sheet of paper.

• Find a Scripture to match each problem. For finances, for example, it might be Philippians 4:19 ('*And my God shall supply all your need according to His riches in glory by Christ Jesus*'); for healing it might be Psalm 107:20 ('*He sent His word and healed them, and delivered them from their destructions*'); and so on.

• Throw the sheet of paper with all your worries in the rubbish bin.

• Start speaking the answer, the Word of God, rather than the problems.

Write out the Scriptures you've found. Put them on the fridge. Take them with you. Put them on tape. Wash yourself in the Word of God and you will find it washes you. 'Worry' on God's Word and the answer will come to pass.

If you stay in God's Word day and night, there is no way that fear will be able to rise again and take up its former dominant position in your heart. There will be too much faith in there!

CHAPTER 10

WINNING WORDS FOR THE BATTLE

The heart of the wise teaches his mouth, and adds learning to his lips.
(Proverbs 16:23)

We live in a world that is spiralling towards great distress. Human beings have tried to solve their own problems and failed. There is not one government on earth today that is not facing some sort of crisis. It's not governments that can solve the ills of the world. It's only the true church, made up of those who confess and know Jesus as Saviour and Lord.

Today a great revival is coming in people's hearts as they discover the Word of God for themselves. Its truth and beauty are bringing hope back into broken lives. But we will only be able to contribute to the victory of God in the world when we have won the battle over our own minds and bodies. That battle is won when we are in control of our lives through God being in control of us.

How we act in times of trouble indicates what has been established in our hearts. Trained soldiers are always ready for battle; when the actual day of fighting comes they don't panic but systematically do what they are trained to do. If they follow the procedures to the letter there is a fair chance they will make it through.

God has established a battle plan for us that guarantees a 100% success rate if we follow His procedures.

With God the odds are far higher. God has established a battle plan for us that guarantees a 100 per cent success rate if we follow His procedures. It's too late to try to find out what the plan is when the battle begins. If we are ignorant of the correct procedures, we will definitely be defeated.

THE GOOD FIGHT OF FAITH

So many Christians wring their hands in grief and despair when tragedy strikes. They don't know how to fight their way through to solid ground and victory.

God says the fight of faith is a good fight, and He wants us to win. He has prepared a strategy guaranteed to defeat every kind of sickness, distress or poverty sent our way by our enemy, the devil. That strategy is faith. We need to use our faith to combat these packages from hell.

If we act in faith we will be powerful. But if we act in fear we will be pitiful.

The irony is that so many Christians believe their battle is really against God. They think it's Him who sends them tragedy. I felt this way myself once when my third baby miscarried. In my grief, I tried to accept the teaching I had at the time that it was God's will for my baby to die. I tried to thank God for taking my baby, because obviously He knew what was best for me. The truth, however, was that I had been robbed of my baby by the thief who comes to rob, kill and destroy. Later I came to see that God only gives us good and perfect gifts.

God allows us to go through these battles, for He knows that as long as the earth remains we will be at war with the forces of darkness. But He equips us with a powerful spiritual weapon: His Word. Against this the enemy has no counter-attack. God's Word is our 'sword of the Spirit' with which we are able to overcome every work of the enemy—if we know how to use it.

It is not enough to pit our natural strength against the devil. We see how deeply this is lacking if we try to overcome cancer or drug addiction, despair or a broken marriage with our limited resources. Only God's weapon (His Word) exercised according to His strategy (faith) can overcome the adversity that Satan brings when he tries to rob, kill and destroy our lives.

Only God's weapon (His Word) used according to His strategy (faith) can overcome the adversity Satan brings.

The Key to Victory

We have seen repeatedly in this book that our beliefs govern our actions. We only act on what we truly believe in our hearts, not what we might think in our minds.

We may want to drive over a rickety bridge after a violent storm, but there is no way we will race across without first assessing whether it can take our car's weight. If we are not fully convinced, there is a fair chance we will back up and find another way around. But if we come to a solid-looking concrete structure, we don't even hesitate. We know such a bridge will take our car's weight easily, and we would be very surprised if it did not.

When we have our hearts firmly established and are trusting in God, we are able to confidently cross all types of bridges in our lives, rickety or not, with absolute confidence. What we believe we will do—nothing more, nothing less. What we sow we will reap—nothing more, nothing less.

There is nothing in this earthly realm that cannot be changed through the injection of God's Word.

It is the Word of God that builds this firm, established heart-faith in our lives. As we speak and declare all the things that God's Word says about us, the battle goes our way. It's not mind over matter; it's God's Word over the devil's circumstances. God's Word has the creative power in it to destroy all the works of the enemy. There is nothing in this earthly realm that cannot be changed through God's Word.

In some ways we are like the Ark of the Covenant. The Word of God once resided gloriously in the Ark and was ceremoniously carried everywhere the Israelites went. If they gave attention to His Word and kept it before them day and night, they were assured of victory in every battle they faced, for God was with them in the presence of that Word.

We are the temple of the Holy Spirit, and if we keep God's Word going into our spirit and coming out of our mouth until it comes to pass, we too will have victory.

> *If you abide in Me, and My words abide in you, you will ask what you desire, and it shall be done for you. By this My Father is glorified, that you bear much fruit. (John 15:7)*

A BATTLE ON MANY FRONTS

The battle we face comes on many fronts, but we meet all the devil's attacks in the same way: through the Word of God, spoken and acted on in faith. When we speak God's Word, we are declaring to the devil that we are aware of our covenant with God and are trusting Him to fulfil His promises.

Here are some of the battle fronts on which we fight.

Living day-by-day. God's strategy is a daily one. We are to start our day with Him and ask His Holy Spirit to guide us through the day.

Then we seek to always act in step with God and not our own self. The businessman asks God to give him insight. The housewife needs God's grace to do all the tasks that await her. The student asks God to enlighten his understanding. The sick and defeated actively work to hear and read the Word so that faith can rise in them to help them out of their sick beds. We all need God every moment.

In the course of each day we will have many opportunities to choose how we are going to act. When the boss reprimands us, will we try to avenge ourselves? If we are hurt and wounded by false accusations, will we turn the other cheek and walk away in forgiveness? If we are tempted to cheat on our tax return, will we juggle the figures? If we are given too much change, will we give it back?

How we act in these cases is an indication of our true character and what is really in our hearts.

Integrity. It's never enough just to hear the Word; we have to *do* it for it to have effect. Words can be cheap if there are no corresponding actions to establish them in our lives.

'I'll give you a call' is devoid of power if we don't make the call we promised. 'I'll try and come' is paramount to saying we won't be there if we don't intend to go. 'It's a deal' is no good if we don't carry out our part of the bargain. Satan, the father of lies, will do all he can to get us to compromise our truthfulness. But when we lie we deceive ourselves, and others will deceive us in turn.

If we always speak truly, even if it is to our loss, we will find our words gain in power. True power comes not from the promise given but from the fulfilment of that promise.

A word here about those who, like me, preach and teach God's Word. So many people would rather see a sermon than hear a sermon. Those who try to preach or teach without leading the life they preach about will be empty of any power or spiritual authority to impact lives.

True power comes not from the promise you give but from the fulfilment of that promise.

The world is quick to point out hypocrisy. Many dead churches have had pulpits filled by leaders whose words have been loveless and lifeless, spoken from their intellect and reasoning. I believe no one can preach or teach anything without the reality of that truth in their own hearts. There is a price to pay to preach to others, and that price is the life we live:

> *In all things [show] yourself to be a pattern of good works; in doctrine [show] integrity, reverence, incorruptibility, sound speech that cannot be condemned, that one who is an opponent may be ashamed, having nothing evil to say of you.* (Titus 2:7–8)

Relationships. None of us are islands living unto ourselves. How we live and what we say affects others.

'A wholesome tongue is a tree of life' (Proverbs 15:4). Our words will create for others either a positive to which they can faithfully aspire or a negative in which they will fearfully remain trapped.

If we tell others they are no good and will never amount to anything, we simply reinforce their old hurts and rejections and consolidate their poor self-image. Alternatively, if we encourage others to be the best and go for the best, we feed them the necessary food they need to build a good self-image and healthy self-esteem. Everyone needs someone to believe in them.

We see this clearly in marriage. Words can either enhance a marriage or destroy it. We can constantly tell our spouse they are boring, useless and no good, and generally point out their faults at every opportunity; but if we do, we are destined for the disaster of divorce.

Every person needs love, support and encouragement, even when they don't seem to be fulfilling the expectations others have for them. To encourage someone is to love them.

Love in the world usually comes with strings attached. Often it's dependent on what can be gained from loving another. Security, wealth, power, esteem—the motives are as varied as people's needs. Once the object of someone's love can no longer meet their need, love is withdrawn. How sad it is to talk with teenagers who feel their lower than expected grades have resulted in a lack of affection and acceptance by their parents. Instead of knowing they are loved for who they are rather than what they can do, they feel pressured to perform at levels far beyond their capacities.

To love someone when the going is not so good is a wonderful, God kind of love.

To love someone when the going is not so good is a wonderful, God kind of love—a love free of ulterior motive or desire for personal gain.

Wise speech. The wicked use speech like glaze over a damaged pot to cover up what is in their heart:

> *He who hates, disguises it with his lips, and lays up deceit within himself; when he speaks kindly, do not believe him ... Though his hatred is covered by deceit, his wickedness will be revealed before the assembly. (Proverbs 26:24–26)*

The wicked person talks primarily from his mind, full of cunning and deceit, with his own interests paramount.

The fool, on the other hand, has no control over his speech:

> *The words of a wise man's mouth are gracious, but the lips of a fool shall swallow him up. (Ecclesiastes 10:12)*

If he feels angry he talks angry. If he is upset with someone he tears them down. Primarily he speaks from his uncontrolled emotions.

In contrast, we need to be wise and speak words that come from our heart, not just our head; from our spirit, not just our emotions. Our 'spirit man' knows exactly what we need to say.

> *The heart of the wise teaches his mouth, and adds learning to his lips. (Proverbs 16:23)*

As Christians, our words too can be tinged with the voice of the world and the flesh. But if our mind is being renewed according to the way God thinks, we will find we can no longer speak principally from how we think and feel.

> *But now you yourselves are to put off all these: anger, wrath, malice, blasphemy, filthy language out of your mouth. (Colossians 3:8)*

Where once we may have had a problem with critical gossip, now we are learning not to engage in that, or even to listen to the rumours that fuel its fire.

Where once we may have spoken without first considering our words and their effect on ourselves and others, now we are learning to discern the time to speak and the time to remain silent.

Where once we may have allowed our mouths to run on, forgetting that '*in the multitude of words sin is not lacking*' (Proverbs 10:19), now we are learning it's good policy not to speak too much. Those who speak from the heart speak fewer words with greater impact.

We need to speak words that come from our hearts, not just our heads.

Where once our words may have given us cause for many regrets, now we are learning that guarding our speech means less that we have to retract or repent of later. Giving attention to God's Word will save us from many days of regret and recrimination.

> *Whoever guards his mouth and tongue keeps his soul from troubles. (Proverbs 21:23)*

THE GREATEST BATTLE

When all is said and done, the greatest battle of all is the fight for the hearts and allegiances of men and women. And the greatest use of our words is to tell others about the good things God has done in our lives.

The greatest use of our words is to tell others about the good things God has done in us.

Whether it's those who know Him as Father or those who are still cut off from Him by sin, our testimony will encourage others to believe God for themselves. He is no respecter of persons. What He has done in our lives He will do in theirs, if they invite Him to.

No one who found a cure for cancer would keep it quiet. We have the cure for all the ills of humankind, and we too can't keep quiet. We are called to be light to a world in darkness and preserving salt to a world in decay. If we hide our light under a bushel, we will not be able to light the way home for those who will never know the way unless we show and tell them.

As God's children we are winners in life, and we will remain winners if we keep our hearts and minds centred on His Word. It's time to take back everything the enemy has stolen from us and see the Body of Christ rise to boldly take God's Word out to the nations.

We will remain winners in life if we keep our hearts and minds centred on God's Word.

The Word of God, revealed by

the Holy Spirit to us, is God's plan for us. We need to read this plan, speak this plan and act on this plan so that we step out into a winning life in every area.

The choice is yours. If you have never done so, begin now by asking Jesus Christ into your life to start the wonderful walk to glory. He is seeking you. He wants you. Today, by an act of your will, you can accept His invitation to a glorious life here on earth, and after that eternal life in His presence forever.

Choose your words; claim your promises; declare your stand in God today. Get His winning words coming out of your mouth. Fight your battles in His strength. Speak your way to health, wealth and prosperity, remembering that true prosperity is everything that death can't take from you.

If you talk like a winner you will walk like a winner. You have God's Word for it!

(You will find the 'Prayer of Salvation' on page 154.)

Some of the Scriptures That Changed My Life

Say it (Proverbs 18:21)—*Hear it* (Romans 10:17)—*It will come to pass* (Mark 11:23)

Power of Words

God says	*You say*
1 Thessalonians 5:23 Now may the God of peace Himself sanctify you completely; and may your whole spirit, soul, and body be preserved blameless at the coming of our Lord Jesus Christ.	'I am a spirit, I live in a body and I have a soul (which is the area of the mind).'
2 Corinthians 4:16 Therefore we do not lose heart. Even though our outward man is perishing, yet the inward man is being renewed day by day.	'Though my outward man is perishing, yet my inward man is being renewed day by day.'
Romans 10:17 So then faith comes by hearing, and hearing by the word of God.	'My words are life and health to me because they are God's words. My words are faith and victory.'
Philippians 4:13 I can do all things through Christ who strengthens me.	'I can do all things through Christ who strengthens me.'
Proverbs 18:21 Death and life are in the power of the tongue, and those who love it will eat its fruit.	'I have faith in my words. What I speak shall come to pass because my words are God's words.'
	'I am bold, I am courageous, I am more than a conqueror and an overcomer.'

SAY IT—HEAR IT—IT WILL COME TO PASS

WORDS CREATE YOUR WORLD

God says	*You say*
Psalm 119:89 Forever, O Lord, Your Word is settled in heaven.	'The Word of God is settled forever. Therefore I establish His Word upon the earth.' 'I base my faith on what God says in His Word.' 'My faith is no higher than my confession.'
Psalm 103:5 Bless the Lord, O my soul, and forget not all His benefits . . . Who satisfies your mouth with good things, so that your youth is renewed like the eagle's.	'God fills my mouth with good things so that my youth is renewed like the eagle's.'
Hebrews 11:3 By faith we understand that the worlds were framed by the word of God, so that the things which are seen were not made of things which are visible.	'My world is framed by my words. My words are God's words.'
2 Corinthians 4:18 . . . we do not look at the things which are seen, but at the things which are not seen. For the things which are seen are temporary, but the things which are not seen are eternal.	'The things which are seen in my life are temporary. They are subject to change.'
Hebrews 13:15 Therefore by Him let us continually offer the sacrifice of praise to God, that is, the fruit of our lips, giving thanks to His name.	'God's Word is continually on my lips. God is my source, He is my strength.' 'I continually give thanks to God by confessing what God says. He and His Word are one.'

SAY IT—HEAR IT—IT WILL COME TO PASS

YOUR MIND CONTROLS YOUR LIFE

God says	*You say*
Romans 8:2 For the law of the Spirit of life in Christ Jesus has made me free from the law of sin and death.	'I am free from the law of sin and death. Jesus made me free.'
Psalm 91:16 With long life I will satisfy him, and show him My salvation.	'I have long life and God's salvation.'
Isaiah 26:3 You will keep him in perfect peace, whose mind is stayed on You, because he trusts in You.	'My mind is stayed on the Word and is in perfect peacc.'
1 Corinthians 2:16 For 'who has known the mind of the Lord that he may instruct Him?' But we have the mind of Christ.	'I have the mind of Christ.'
Romans 12:2 And do not be conformed to this world, but be transformed by the renewing of your mind, that you may prove what is that good and acceptable and perfect will of God.	'I am transformed by the renewing of my mind.'
Philippians 4:8 Finally, brethren, whatever things are true, whatever things are noble, whatever things are just, whatever things are pure, whatever things are lovely, whatever things are of good report, if there is any virtue and if there is anything praiseworthy—meditate on these things.	'I think on true things, pure things, holy things, lovely things, things of good report. I think on God's Word. His promises are mine.'

SAY IT—HEAR IT—IT WILL COME TO PASS

SELF-IMAGE

God says	*You say*
John 1:12–13 But as many as received Him, to them He gave the right to become children of God, to those who believe in His name: who were born, not of blood, nor of the will of the flesh, nor of the will of man, but of God.	'I am born of God.'
2 Corinthians 5:17 Therefore, if anyone is in Christ, he is a new creation; old things have passed away: behold, all things have become new.	'I am a new creation in Christ. My past is wiped out. It's gone. Jesus took it.'
1 John 4:4 He who is in you is greater than he who is in the world.	'He who is in me is greater than he who is in the world.'
Psalm 103:5 Bless the Lord, O my soul, and forget not all His benefits . . . Who satisfies your mouth with good things, so that your youth is renewed like the eagle's.	'I satisfy my mouth with good things so that my youth is renewed like the eagle's.' (Eagles have long life. They cast off their old feathers and receive new ones. We need to cast off our old habits and thoughts and receive anew from God's Word. The old will die and new life will come.)
Galatians 2:20 I have been crucified with Christ; it is no longer I who live, but Christ lives in me; and the life which I now live in the flesh I live by faith in the Son of God, who loved me and gave Himself for me.	'It's not I that live, but Christ lives within me. He sees me as valuable and precious.'

SAY IT—HEAR IT—YOU WILL BELIEVE IT

FAITH ACTS

God says	*You say*
Psalm 46:1 God is our refuge and strength, a very present help in trouble.	'God, you are an ever present help in the midst of trouble.'
Philippians 4:19 And my God shall supply all your need according to His riches in glory by Christ Jesus.	'My God shall supply all my needs according to His riches in glory by Christ Jesus.'
Proverbs 3:5 Trust in the Lord with all your heart, and lean not on your own understanding.	'I trust in the Lord with all my heart and lean not on my own understanding.'
1 Peter 5:7 . . . casting all your care upon Him, for He cares for you.	'I cast all my cares upon Him, for He cares for me.'
James 1:22 But be doers of the word, and not hearers only, deceiving yourselves.	'I am a doer of the Word, not a hearer only.'
Romans 10:17 So then faith comes by hearing, and hearing by the word of God.	'"Faith comes by hearing, and hearing by the word of God." My words are faith because they are God's words. My words are grace to the hearers. My words are health because they are God's words.'

SAY IT—HEAR IT—YOU WILL BELIEVE IT

JESUS OUR HEALER

God says	*You say*
Proverbs 4:22 For they [God's words] are life to those who find them, and health to all their flesh.	'The Word of God is life to me and health to all my flesh.'
Psalm 107:20 He sent His word and healed them, and delivered them from their destructions.	'He sent His Word and healed me, and delivered me from my destructions (growth or whatever the sickness is). Healing belongs to me.' 'Thank You, Jesus, that I am healed, for your Word says I'm healed.'
Isaiah 53:5 But He was wounded for our transgressions, He was bruised for our iniquities; the chastisement for our peace was upon Him, and by His stripes we are healed.	'He was wounded for my transgressions, He was bruised for my iniquities; the chastisement for my peace was upon Him, and by His stripes I am healed.'
Matthew 8:17 He Himself took our infirmities and bore our sicknesses.	'He Himself took my infirmities and bore my sicknesses. Jesus took sickness 2000 years ago for me to walk in divine health.'
Mark 11:23 For assuredly, I say to you, whoever says to this mountain, 'Be removed and be cast into the sea,' and does not doubt in his heart, but believes that those things he says will be done, he will have whatever he says.	Sickness is the mountain. Call it by name—flu, cancer, growth, back trouble, whatever it is—and tell it, 'Be removed, in Jesus' name!'
1 Peter 2:24 . . . by whose stripes you were healed.	'Sickness, you have no place in my body. The life of God is in me, His healing power is flowing through me. God's Word says I am healed, so I am.'
Romans 10:17 So then faith comes by hearing, and hearing by the word of God.	'My words are faith because they are God's words. Healing belongs to me. Jesus paid the price for me on the Cross, and I have long life and His salvation.'

SAY IT—HEAR IT—IT WILL COME TO PASS

THE WORD OF GOD IS INNER HEALING

God says	*You say*
2 Corinthians 5:17 Therefore, if anyone is in Christ, he is a new creation; old things have passed away: behold, all things have become new.	'I am a new creation in Christ Jesus. Old things have passed away and all things have become new!'
1 John 4:4 He who is in you is greater than he who is in the world.	'He who is in me is greater than he who is in the world.' (Christ lives in you.) 'I have His nature in me. His love is shed abroad in my heart. I have His ability in me.'
Galatians 2:20 It is no longer I who live, but Christ lives in me.	'It is no longer I who live, but Christ lives in me.'
Romans 8:37 Yet in all these things we are more than conquerors through Him who loves us.	'I am more than a conqueror through Him who loves me.'
Philippians 4:13 I can do all things through Christ who strengthens me.	'I can do all things through Christ who strengthens me.'
2 Timothy 1:7 For God has not given us a spirit of fear, but of power and of love and of a sound mind.	'I haven't been given a spirit of fear, but of power and of love and of a sound mind.'

JESUS MADE YOU RIGHTEOUS

God says	*You say*
2 Corinthians 5:21 For He made Him who knew no sin to be sin for us, that we might become the righteousness of God in Him.	'For He made Him who knew no sin to be sin for me, that I might become the righteousness of God in Him.' (The Divine Exchange: God put your sins on Jesus and He gave you His righteousness.)
Isaiah 54:14 In righteousness you shall be established; you shall be far from oppression, for you shall not fear; and from terror, for it shall not come near you.	'In righteousness I shall be established; I shall be far from oppression, for I shall not fear; and from terror, for it shall not come near me.' (This righteousness is a gift from God. You can't work for it.)
Matthew 12:37 For by your words you will be justified, and by your words you will be condemned.	'For by my words I will be justified [made righteous], and by my words I will be condemned.' (Say who you are in Christ. Guilt, condemnation, unworthiness, inferiority, sin-consciousness will drop off.)
Romans 5:17 For if by one man's offence death reigned through the one, much more those who receive abundance of grace and of the gift of righteousness will reign in life through the One, Jesus Christ.	'I have abundance of grace and the gift of righteousness through Jesus Christ.'

OVERCOMING SATAN

God says	*You say*
1 John 4:4 You are of God, little children, and have overcome them, because He who is in you is greater than he who is in the world.	'I am of God and I overcome him who is in the world (Satan).'
Ephesians 6:16 . . . above all, taking the shield of faith with which you will be able to quench all the fiery darts of the wicked one.	'I take the shield of faith and I quench every fiery dart that the wicked one brings against me.'
James 4:7 Therefore submit to God. Resist the devil and he will flee from you.	'The devil flees from me because I resist him in the name of Jesus.'
Romans 12:21 Do not be overcome by evil, but overcome evil with good.	'I overcome evil with good.'
Revelation 12:11 And they overcame him [the devil] by the blood of the Lamb and by the word of their testimony, and they did not love their lives to the death.	'I am an overcomer and I overcome by the blood of the Lamb and the word of my testimony.'
2 Thessalonians 3:3 But the Lord is faithful, who will establish you and guard you from the evil one.	'The Lord *is* faithful and He *will* strengthen and protect me from the evil one.'

SAY IT—HEAR IT—IT WILL COME TO PASS

OVERCOMING DEPRESSION

God says	*You say*
2 Timothy 1:7 For God has not given us a spirit of fear, but of power and of love and of a sound mind.	'I haven't been given a spirit of fear, but of power and of love and of a *sound mind.*' (He has given you a sound mind. Train your mind to think on God's Word.)
Philippians 4:6–8 Be anxious for nothing, but in everything by prayer and supplication, with thanksgiving, let your requests be made known to God; and the peace of God, which surpasses all understanding, will guard your hearts and minds through Christ Jesus. Finally, brethren, whatever things are true, whatever things are noble, whatever things are just, whatever things are pure, whatever things are lovely, whatever things are of good report, if there is any virtue and if there is anything praiseworthy—meditate on these things.	'I am anxious for nothing, but in everything by prayer and supplication [deep request], with thanksgiving, I let my requests be made known to God.' (He did not say, 'make your problems known', but 'make your requests known'. Cast the care of the problem over to the Lord.) 'And the peace of God, which surpasses all understanding, will guard my heart and mind through Christ Jesus.' 'I think on things that are true, 'I think on things that are noble, 'I think on things that are just, 'I think on things that are pure, 'I think on things that are lovely, 'I think on things that are of good report.'
Romans 12:2 And do not be conformed to this world, but be transformed by the renewing of your mind, that you may prove what is that good and acceptable and perfect will of God.	'I am transformed by the renewing of my mind.'
Psalm 103:5 Bless the Lord, O my soul, and forget not all His benefits . . . Who satisfies your mouth with good things, so that your youth is renewed like the eagle's.	'I satisfy my mouth with good things so that my youth is renewed like the eagle's.'

SAY IT—HEAR IT—YOU WILL BELIEVE IT

OVERCOMING FEAR

God says	*You say*
1 Thessalonians 5:23 Now may the God of peace Himself sanctify you completely; and may your whole spirit, soul, and body be preserved blameless at the coming of our Lord Jesus Christ.	'I am a spirit, I live in a body and I have a soul.' (As you feed the Word of God into your spirit fear will leave.)
Proverbs 4:22 For they [God's words] are life to those who find them, and health to all their flesh.	'The Word of God is life to me and health to all my flesh.' (Your flesh will get in line with your spirit.)
2 Timothy 1:7 For God has not given us a spirit of fear, but of power and of love and of a sound mind.	'I haven't been given a spirit of fear, but of power and of love and of a sound mind.'
Romans 8:15 For you did not receive the spirit of bondage again to fear, but you received the Spirit of adoption by whom we cry out, 'Abba, Father.'	'I haven't been given a spirit of bondage again to fear, but a spirit of adoption by whom I cry out, "Abba, Father".' (When you accepted Jesus as Lord of your life He brought you out of darkness into light.)
Psalm 27:12 The Lord is my light and my salvation; whom shall I fear? The Lord is the strength of my life; of whom shall I be afraid? When the wicked came against me to eat up my flesh, my enemies and foes they stumbled and fell.	'The Lord is my light and my salvation; whom shall I fear? The Lord is the strength of my life; of whom shall I be afraid?'
Isaiah 54:14 In righteousness you shall be established; you shall be far from oppression, for you shall not fear; and from terror, for it shall not come near you.	'I am far from oppression, and fear does not come near me.'
Psalm 23:4 Yea, though I walk through the valley of the shadow of death, I will fear no evil; for You are with me; Your rod and Your staff, they comfort me.	'I will fear no evil, for You are with me, Lord; Your Word and Your Spirit comfort me.'

SAY IT—HEAR IT—YOU WILL BELIEVE IT

OVERCOMING WORRY

God says	*You say*
Matthew 28:20 And lo, I am with you always, even to the end of the age.	'Jesus is with me always.'
Galatians 1:3–4 Grace to you and peace from God the Father and our Lord Jesus Christ, Who gave Himself for our sins, that He might deliver us from this present evil age, according to the will of our God and Father.	'I am delivered from the evils of this present world, for it is the will of God.'
Psalm 91:10–11 No evil shall befall you, nor shall any plague come near your dwelling; for He shall give His angels charge over you, to keep you in all your ways.	'No evil shall befall me, neither shall any plague come near my dwelling. For You have given Your angels charge over me and they keep me in all my ways.'
Proverbs 12:28 In the way of righteousness is life, and in its pathway there is no death.	'In my pathway is life and there is no death.'
Isaiah 54:17 'No weapon formed against you shall prosper, and every tongue which rises against you in judgment you shall condemn. This is the heritage of the servants of the Lord, and their righteousness is from Me,' says the Lord.	'No weapon formed against me shall prosper, for my righteousness is of the Lord.'
Psalm 1:1–2 He [the godly man] shall be like a tree planted by the rivers of water, that brings forth its fruit in its season, whose leaf also shall not wither; and whatever he does shall prosper.	'Whatever I do will prosper because I am like a tree planted by rivers of water.'

SAY IT—HEAR IT—IT WILL COME TO PASS

PRAYING FOR YOUR FAMILY

God says	*You say*
1 John 5:14 Now this is the confidence that we have in Him, that if we ask anything according to His will, He hears us.	'Now this is the confidence that I have in Him, that if I ask anything according to His will, He hears me.'
Joshua 24:15 As for me and my house, we will serve the Lord.	'As for me and my house, we will serve the Lord.'
Isaiah 54:13 All your children shall be taught by the Lord, and great shall be the peace of your children.	'Great is the peace of my children for they are taught of the Lord.'
Unsaved loved ones and others: Ephesians 1:17 . . . that the God of our Lord Jesus Christ, the Father of glory, may give to you the spirit of wisdom and revelation in the knowledge of Him, the eyes of your understanding being enlightened: that you may know what is the hope of His calling, what are the riches of the glory of His inheritance in the saints.	'. . . that the God of our Lord Jesus Christ, the Father of glory, may give to (name of person) the spirit of wisdom and revelation in the knowledge of Him, the eyes of (name of person)'s understanding being enlightened: that (he/she) may know what is the hope of His calling, what are the riches of the glory of His inheritance in the saints.'
Those who are backslidden: Job 22:30 He will even deliver one who is not innocent; yes, he will be delivered by the purity of your hands.	'He will even deliver (name of person for whom you are interceding) who is not innocent; yes, he will be delivered by the purity of my hands.'

SAY IT—HEAR IT—IT WILL COME TO PASS

The Prayer of Salvation

I was number one in the world in tennis. I had money and fame. But there was still something missing in my life. For thirty years I sat in a church pew, but no-one ever told me that I needed to make a decision to ask Jesus Christ into my life as my own personal Saviour and Lord.

The Bible clearly states in Romans 10:9–10: *'If you confess with your mouth the Lord Jesus and believe in your heart that God has raised Him from the dead, you will be saved. For with the heart one believes unto righteousness, and with the mouth confession is made unto salvation.'*

By praying the following prayer, out loud, and believing it in your heart, you will have the same assurance of eternal life that I have today.

> 'Heavenly Father, I believe Jesus is Your Son and that You have raised Him from the dead. I thank You that You have forgiven and forgotten all my past mistakes—that old things have passed away and all things are now new. I am now born again. I have

new life right from this moment. I have eternal life now in the name of Jesus and I thank You for it. Amen.' (2 Corinthians 5:17)

Congratulations, and welcome to the family of God! I urge you to join a Word-based church to grow in the things of God. Please write and tell us of this wonderful decision you have made today.

Victory Life Centre
PO Box 20
Osborne Park WA 6917
Australia
Ph: +61-8-9201-1266. Fax: +61-8-9201-1299
E-mail: mcourt@victorylifecentre.com.au
Web: www.victorylifecentre.com.au

I pray God's peace and protection on you and your family, and pray for success in everything you purpose to do in life.

Margaret Court